**Community Care
Practice Handbooks**

General Editor: Martin Davies

Working With Depressed Women

Community Care Practice Handbooks

General Editor: Martin Davies

Working With Depressed Women

A Feminist Approach

Alison Corob

Gower

Published by
Gower Publishing Company Limited
Gower House
Croft Road
Aldershot
Hants GU11 3HR
England

Gower Publishing Company
Old Post Road
Brookfield
Vermont 05036
USA

British Library Cataloguing in Publication Data

Corob, Alison
  Working with depressed women: a feminist
  approach. — (Community care practice
  handbook; 22)
  1. Social work with women   2. Depression,
  Mental
  I. Title   II. Series
  362.2'0425   HV1444

ISBN 0 566 05100 1 (Pbk)
ISBN 0 566 05424 8 (Hbk)

Printed and bound in Great Britain by
Biddles Ltd, Guildford and King's Lynn

Contents

Acknowledgements

I am greatly indebted to all the women who allowed me to interview them for this book. Their openness, honesty and courage were admirable and strengthened my belief in women's fortitude and ability to survive against all odds. I would also like to thank those agencies, groups and individuals who referred women to me.

I am most grateful to the following friends and colleagues for reading draft chapters and for offering helpful comments and ideas: Jacky Boucherat, Fiona Gardner, Tina Osner and Susan O'Conner. I would also like to thank Sue Eales for her patience and perseverance in typing the manuscript.

Very special thanks goes to Joseph Hajnal, whose sustained and invaluable help and support throughout the many months of writing I could never have done without.

Introduction

This book was born out of a growing awareness of the high proportion of social work clients, particularly female clients, who suffer from depression to some degree or another. Social workers encounter depressed women not only in those cases classified as 'mental health problems' but also in many instances where the presenting problem is defined as something different. However, it is clear that for various reasons the needs of depressed women are frequently not attended to, or even acknowledged, by the social work profession. This failure may in part be attributed to a tendency among social workers to overlook their potential contribution to helping depressed people. Additionally, many social workers lack, or feel that they lack, the skills necessary to help clients who are mentally or emotionally troubled. This is unfortunate, since there is much scope for social work with people with mental health problems.

It is possible that social workers in general will become more conscious of mental health issues as a result of the Mental Health Act 1983, and that some will develop a greater expertise in this area of work. Unfortunately however, the Act only requires local authorities to train and 'approve' a 'sufficient number' of social workers to carry out certain specific duties. Thus it may not provide much stimulus for a general improvement in the quality of care offered by social workers to those with mental health problems such as depression.

It is essential for all social workers, approved or not, to develop skills to deal adequately and appropriately with depressed people. This is important not only because they figure so highly on social work caseloads, but also because these clients do not necessarily go elsewhere for help. If they do, they are most likely to go to GPs who still tend to offer drugs as the treatment of choice for depression. Pills may suppress the symptoms of distress, but they rarely deal with the causes of it. The need for some kind of therapeutic assistance is clear, and social work departments are a good place from which to offer it. Many of the conditions necessary to provide a therapeutically oriented service are already in existence within social work, and need only to be exploited. This is not to underplay the role of doctors, or the importance of cooperation between social workers and doctors, it is rather to stress the point that social workers can make a valuable contribution to helping those with depression.

This book attempts to help social workers become more familiar with the problem of depression and more competent in dealing with it. Ways in which to provide therapeutic as well as practical aid to depressed women are suggested. These may require social workers to extend their repertoire of skills, but they can in large part be achieved simply by adapting those skills already developed through social work training and practice. The focus is on methods designed to help women to overcome their depressions, whilst also offering them a means of increasing their personal power, developing their own potential and generally generating a life-style that may prevent depression recurring in the future. Individual and group methods have been singled out as being most appropriate for these purposes. Marital and family therapies are not discussed, for although they have been shown to be helpful for dealing with relationship difficulties, and hence may help in reducing the risk of future depressions, they are relatively ineffective for relieving the distress of current depressions (Friedman 1975) and for empowering women. Psychiatric emergencies such as suicide attempts or compulsory hospital admissions and the statutory obligations of approved social workers are also beyond the scope of this book. These areas of mental health work are covered elsewhere (see for example Hudson 1982, Butler and Pritchard 1983, Olsen 1984, Huxley 1985).

The focus on women in this book, derives largely from the fact that they are far more likely to get depressed than men. This is not a coincidence, nor due simply to biological factors. It is intimately connected with the roles and status of women in society, and with the ways in which they have been conditioned to adopt these roles. As such, the subject of women and depression is worthy of discussion by social workers and is of import to them. The text explores theories and explanations for women's particular vulnerability to depression, and factors that may make women depressed. This exploration should throw light on issues and dilemmas faced by all women, for the concerns and difficulties experienced by women who get depressed are not usually essentially different from those experienced by women in general.

Our concern with the needs and experiences of women is in no way intended to deny or negate those of men and children. It is simply intended to help social workers to sharpen their awareness of some of the predicaments and problems that particularly affect women. This is necessary because of the relative failure of the social work profession to acknowledge that women's needs and experiences are sometimes quite distinct from those of men. The dimension of gender has a profound impact on life-experiences and options as well as on emotional states and behaviour. Its significance, however, has consistently been underrated in both social work theory and practice.

The concentration on women, and the acknowledgement of their experiences as important and valid, lend the book a feminist perspective. Quotations from depressed, or previously depressed women (extracted from 25 taped interviews) play a central role in the text, illustrating and highlighting the points raised. The book may also be deemed feminist because it acknowledges the social and economic inequalities which women suffer in relation to men, and because it links their intensely personal experiences of depression with social and political factors. An exploration of issues from this perspective forms the starting point from which to develop a feminist social work practice. The book considers how social workers can integrate a feminist analysis into their practice and act on it for the benefit of women in general and depressed women in particular.

Feminist-oriented social work is necessary not simply because of the needs of female clients, but also because of current sex-biased policies and practices which tend to ignore or repudiate these needs. Of course the existence of such policies may make it difficult for social workers to adopt a feminist perspective in their work. Notwithstanding these difficulties social workers should find that feminist social work provides an effective means of meeting the needs of depressed women.

Inevitably, the book leaves much unsaid. In terms of women's lives and viewpoints, it portrays a range of different life-experiences and perspectives, but of necessity, does not capture the full diversity and complexity that exists. Similarly, a range of social work strategies and techniques that may be useful to depressed women and that can be incorporated into a feminist perspective are discussed, but these are not intended to constitute the entirety of methods available. However, it is hoped that this book will contribute to the development of a social work practice that is more responsive to the needs of women and to all people with mental health problems.

1 Social Work, Medical Practice and Depression

In this chapter we begin by establishing the relevance of depression to social workers. We go on to consider the signs and symptoms of depression and to make a critical appraisal of medical diagnoses, methods and treatments, including drugs and electroconvulsive therapy (ECT). The role of the social worker will be discussed in relation to both the medical team and to clients themselves. Women's own experiences and views about the various matters under consideration are interspersed throughout the chapter.

Social work and depression

Depression is part and parcel of social work; it crops up again and again in the individuals and families that social workers see in the course of their work. Whether they are placed in the statutory or voluntary sectors, in hospitals, clinics or the community, social workers are bound to come face to face with women suffering from depression. Research suggests that it is a widespread problem — 10–15 per cent of the British population may suffer from depression at some time in their lives. It is at least twice as common in women as it is in men and most prevalent in lower socio-economic groups, where it tends to go unrecognized and untreated (Brown and Harris 1978). Since those people who go to welfare agencies are, almost by definition, experiencing some difficulty in their lives and tend, moreover to be women and working-class, the proportion of social work clients who are depressed is likely to be very high indeed. Studies of Social Services Departments (SSDs) clients provide some support for this contention (Huxley and Fitzpatrick 1984).

Depression can be found in almost any client group with which social workers have contact — adolescents, 'child-abusing' parents, disabled or elderly people and so on — although it is rarely the primary cause for referral. Depression can also be seen in a more hidden group — that of the carers of these clients. Behind such cases defined as 'child-care', 'elderly' or 'handicapped' will be women, as mothers, wives or daughters, who are contending with the daily realities of looking after dependent and sometimes difficult children or relatives. Continually meeting the demands of others is wearing and stressful, and such women will doubtless be struggling to maintain a fine balance between coping and collapse. Breakdown may be held off by the consumption of tranquillizers, but the stressful nature of their lives will remain. The so-called 'inadequate mothers' of child-care cases or 'uncaring daughters' of the elderly may need help as people in their own right. Social workers must therefore sensitize themselves to the problems of distress and depression in all the women of their caseloads, and be ready to respond accordingly. They must relinquish the belief that the medical professions hold a monopoly over depressed people, or that such a group are only of marginal interest to social workers who are not approved or to those working outside psychiatric hospitals. They need to confront the problem of depression head on, and be prepared to deal with it.

Social workers are in a prime position to offer assistance to depressed people, for social and psychosocial factors play such a major role in the development and maintenance of most depressions. The social work perspective, with its broad knowledge base, can be of immense value to the understanding, as well as to the treatment of depression. The social workers' role means that they can intervene at any one of several levels — at the level of the individual, the family and/or the community. Unlike most other professionals, social workers are in a position to attend to both the inner *and* outer needs of clients, to offer therapeutic help as well as practical assistance.

Studies of social workers working alongside GPs suggest that when care is taken to attend to both the practical and emotional needs of depressed people social workers can indeed make a valuable contribution to alleviating depression (Cooper *et al* 1975; Shepherd *et al* 1979; Corney and Clare 1983). However, it seems that a large proportion of social workers, particularly those in district SSDs, tend to concentrate their efforts almost entirely on giving practical and material assistance to 'mentally ill' clients. It is less common for them to offer structured therapeutic help that aims to create change

(Fisher *et al* 1984). This may be because of inadequate training which could cause social workers to feel ill-equipped and unconfident about dealing effectively with mental health problems. They may consequently attempt to relegate such problems to a subsidiary position, preferring to deal with other difficulties. Clients themselves have sometimes spoken of their disappointment at the lack of attention given by social workers to their distress and depression (Fisher *et al* 1984). It is essential therefore, to redress the balance and ensure that social workers develop therapeutic skills suitable for helping depressed people.

The signs and symptoms of depression

To be able to assess whether a person is suffering from depression social workers have to know what signs and symptoms to look for. Although most of these are obvious and familiar, there are some that are more subtle and may get overlooked or be identified as other problems. Social workers need to be aware of these because people do not always recognise for themselves that they are depressed. This is not to suggest that a woman's own judgement is insignificant, but merely that one problem can mask another.

Depression is a complex phenomenon, and one that can affect people in different ways. It usually produces a constellation of symptoms, affecting an individual's feelings, thoughts and behaviour. Which particular symptoms are present will vary from one person to another. Feelings may range from sadness, low self-esteem, helplessness, hopelessness or pessimism, to total despair and a sense of utter worthlessness or futility. There may also be feelings of intense guilt, anxiety and irritability. Thoughts generally centre around themes of self-deprecation, possibly suicide and sometimes fears of severe illness. Thinking itself may become difficult and concentration impaired. A person may become totally self-absorbed, be unable to take pleasure in anything, including sexual activity, and find themselves completely apathetic and lacking in energy. Sleep and appetite disturbances (either sleeping/eating too much or too little) and physical symptoms, such as aches and pains, may well also be present. Finally, there may be a heightening of already existing personality characteristics, so that a person might become, for example, more obsessional, phobic or anxious.

These symptoms of depression are usually no more than an exaggeration of so-called 'normal' feeling states. Indeed, the utter sense of self-hatred, worthlessness and inadequacy that we see in depressed women, is merely an intensification of the way so many women feel about themselves much of the time. To really understand what it feels like to be deeply depressed however, we must listen to what those who have suffered in this way have to say about it. Here are some quotations from women talking about what depression feels like and how it affects them:

When I was depressed I couldn't sleep, couldn't eat, couldn't go out or stay in, I just used to cry an awful lot, I'm not sure what about — bills, money, life in general I think.

Depression's very frightening. You feel as if someone's chucked you in this great big pit and put a lid on and you can't get out — there's no way to get out and I don't know what's happening.

When I'm depressed my mind goes so fast I don't know what I'm thinking and I can't sleep.

One of the symptoms of my depression was this terrible suicide wish, there was this utter hopelessness, you think you'll never pick up and you feel so very very ill all the time and you get no relief from it whatsoever. Everyday you wake up and feel ill, nothing is worth doing and you get no pleasure from anything at all – no books, no T.V., no laughter; the sun only mocks you, the flowers mean nothing, nothing means anything to you at all ... you exist but you don't live.

When I'm depressed it's like having a huge great black cloud sitting on me and over me and I just sit and cry.

When you're depressed you feel really ill and you don't know what you're doing, you get carried away and get irritable and worked up. I felt sick, I had no energy to do anything, I felt tired all the time and wanted to cry all the time, and anyone can upset me if they say the slightest thing.

When I'm depressed I get agoraphobic and eat all the time.

I felt I was in the wrong, I was a failure, and a lousy person. I felt ugly and fat and evil.

I feel guilty about everyone and everything even if it doesn't concern me. I think everything's all my fault, I blame myself even if no-one else does.

I felt I was out of my head, totally out of control and I didn't know what to do next. I had to live minute by minute, not knowing what the next half-hour would bring ... I couldn't bear to think about being in the world ... everything was happening around me and I was just a very small part. I just didn't have a sense of belonging in the world. I felt completely alone, with no-one to talk to and couldn't see the point of being alive.

My picture of depression is of emptiness and bleakness and blackness and total acceptance of the situation with no struggle whatsoever.

Sometimes when I'm depressed I just withdraw and sit and stare into space ... I get very apathetic and sometimes I can't breathe properly, just very shallowly. I'm a real pain in the arse to be with.

I see depression now as anger turned against myself because I can't express anger.

When I'm depressed I think I'm so revolting I don't deserve to have anyone care for me, I deserve to be beaten up, because I'm so worthless that what does it matter anyway? ... Once I'm down it's so hard to get up because I feel so worthless that people could just walk all over me, and they do because I let them, I don't fight, and then I feel even worse about myself.

Depression affected my body — one part of it didn't work properly, it felt paralysed. It also used to shake all the time and I had no energy. It affected my brain too — I couldn't think anything, only that I was going to die. At first I didn't realise it was depression.

When I'm depressed I also get very anxious about everything and have panic attacks when I go out shopping.

I feel so miserable that I feel like I'm falling down a really deep pit and I keep grabbing on to the sides, but because I'm running out of strength the sides break off and I keep falling, and then I'm sitting at the bottom terrified 'cause I think how am I going to get out and get on with life?

Medical definitions of depression

Those suffering from the symptoms of depression generally turn to the medical services if they need professional help. Since social workers are likely to be working alongside the medical professions, or working with women who have had contact with them at some time, it is essential for social workers to be familiar with psychiatric diagnoses and treatments. Such familiarity should not only make social workers more assertive in dealing with doctors, but also help them to help their clients, who may need labels and diagnoses explained or interpreted. Knowledge of such diagnoses might also help social workers feel more confident in their own assessments. However, there is no need for them to subscribe entirely to medical models of mental illness, for there are significant limitations to this approach, which we will discuss later in the chapter. Also, the concerns of the social worker are different from those of the doctor.

The classification of 'depression' is a controversial subject among psychiatrists. Some regard it as a single disorder, while others consider that there are different types of depression which have distinct causes and symptoms and require different approaches to treatment. Three different diagnostic schemes are commonly used:

Endogenous – reactive

Endogenous means arising from within and refers to a depression apparently developing spontaneously. The cause is generally considered to be certain bio-chemical processes in the brain. The term endogenous is more likely to be applied to those with a high proportion of physical symptoms. Reactive depressions are those brought about by identifiable events or traumas in a person's life, usually loss or stress.

This distinction does not always work well in practice. Depressions may be diagnosed as endogenous for lack of an obvious external trauma or particular stress with which to associate their onset. However, there may be internal conflicts or other 'unfinished business' related to past events which have only recently been given overt expression. In reactive depression there may be physiological processes which are precipitated by the traumatic emotional state.

> I was told I had an endogenous depression which I found out later was a depression that comes out of the blue and has no obvious cause. Well I felt the cause was obvious, I had plenty of explanations for it. But they just thought I was over-reacting I suppose.

Anthony Clare contends that many psychiatrists are 'too busy to do more than undertake a cursory examination of their patient's history and mental state'. Accordingly, they 'diagnose an excessive number of depressions as arising "out of the blue"' (i.e. as endogenous) (Clare 1980 p. 251).

Psychotic – neurotic

This distinction closely resembles the previous one, but here the emphasis is on whether or not the individual is in contact with 'reality' and on their perceived distance from 'normality' (Hudson 1982). Someone with a psychotic depression might have delusions and hallucinations, be convinced that she is guilty and wicked, and lack insight into the nature and cause of the problem. Neurotic depressions are usually situationally produced and contact with 'reality' is maintained.

In practice this division may again be blurred. The distinction between 'reality' and 'unreality' or 'sanity' and 'insanity' is by no means clear cut.

Severe – mild

A severely depressed person may be defined as someone who is unable to look after herself, whose general health is suffering and who may be at risk of self-injury or suicide. She may have psychotic symptoms, be stuporous, or extremely agitated. Depressive episodes may remain mild or severe or progress from one to the other.

The terms endogenous, psychotic and severe are sometimes treated as equivalents, although, as Hudson (1982) comments, an endogenous depression need not be severe, though a psychotic one always is. Reactive or neurotic depression can be severe.

There are other forms of depression which may be alluded to. Here are a few of the many labels that may be ascribed:

Manic – *depressive psychosis*
Usually this term applies to people suffering from dramatic swings of mood. These alternate between periods of depression, which may lead to complete withdrawal from normal activity, to episodes of mania, which involve excitement, euphoria and compulsive activity or talking. Sometimes one mood will be closely followed by another, at other times, there will be periods of stability in between. Sometimes the term is used synonymously with endogenous or psychotic depression, in which case it will be called the 'uni-polar' (just depression) rather than the 'bi-polar' (depression and mania) type of manic-depressive psychosis.

Bi-polar manic-depression is less common than the uni-polar type, and incidence rates are almost equal for men and women. There is good evidence to suggest that it is genetically induced. In this book the problem of manic-depression will not be addressed specifically, although there may be points and issues raised that are relevant to it.

Agitated depression
In this form of depression the person also experiences much anxiety with its attendant symptoms of insomnia, tension, restlessness and possibly panic attacks.

Clinical depression
This term usually implies a depression that is serious enough to require treatment, an illness rather than a mood.

Where to draw the line between illness and mood, or serious and not serious, is unclear. It is the author's opinion that depression ranges along a continuum, in terms of depth and severity, as well as the extent to which physical, psychological and emotional functioning is impaired. There is not one point at which a depression becomes 'clinical'.

It is clear that psychiatric diagnoses lack clarity and that they are not applied uniformly by doctors. What is an endogenous depression to one is a psychotic or clinical depression to another. Furthermore, there is little consensus as to what constitutes a particular disorder, so that an individual may be told variously, that she has a psychotic or neurotic depression, schizophrenia, or a personality disorder.

The problem of accurate diagnosis is further complicated when doctors are dealing with people from different cultures. If a doctor does not understand the language, culture and customs of an individual they may misdiagnose as 'mentally ill' what is in fact 'normal' and acceptable behaviour in a particular culture. Such misinterpretation has occasionally led to the inappropriate sectioning of people from ethnic minorities (CRE 1976).

Psychiatric diagnoses become labels which tend to remain fixed and rigid. People then feel that they can never be rid of these labels and the stigma attached to them.

> They told me I had a personality disorder and a clinical depression. This made me feel that there was something wrong with me that would never go away and that I would be labelled 'mental' for life. Really I think I was just very unhappy...

> Once you've been labelled as mentally ill in some way, that's it for life, it's as if you can never change, because you always have to declare it on job forms and things like that.

In addition, labels conspire to further divide people from each other. Ruth Elizabeth explains the effects of labelling on her, and so-called 'normal' women:

> I really do feel separated off, as if behind some sort of enclosure, from most of the women I know. Partly, this is the result of having been labelled 'mentally ill' and made to feel unfit to mingle with the rest of the world, so that it is very hard for me now to believe that I am acceptable, that I have a right to be here. But I also believe that this sense of separateness is perpetuated, perhaps unwittingly by other women who distance themselves from me (Elizabeth 1983 p. 19).

The diagnosis applied to an individual by a doctor tends to

determine the treatment offered and the role of other professionals. Those who are diagnosed as having a reactive, neurotic or mild depression will generally be prescribed psychotropic (mood altering) drugs and later, possibly electro-convulsive therapy (ECT). They may also be referred to social workers who may occasionally be asked to take a prominent role in such cases. People believed to have psychotic, endogenous, or severe depressions will generally be considered to warrant only drugs or ECT. However, as we shall see, these treatments tend to be inefficient and inexpedient.

Given the uncertainty of psychiatric diagnoses and the in-efficiency of much of the treatment, social workers would be advised to make their own assessments and should be willing to offer a complementary, if not alternative, service to their clients. They should try to ensure that all those who can benefit from and want a talking therapy are offered it, either by themselves or other members of the team. When appropriate they need to be prepared to challenge, as well as collaborate with, medical definitions and decisions about treatment. Close and smooth cooperation between professionals may seem an excellent idea in theory; in practice, it can mean simply agreeing with, or following the judgement and advice of doctors. In fact, inter-disciplinary friction may often lead to a more thorough examination of the problem and consequently to a more fruitful decision about treatment. Any independent interventions by social workers must of course be based on a thorough and working knowledge of the matter in hand. However, even with such expertise, the greater power, prestige and usually assumed authority of medics, means that it will not always be easy for social workers to influence the processes of decision-making. They will need to have confidence as well as expertise, and pre-ferably also support from their department and other pro-fessionals.

Doctors and the medical model

The medical model, in which the practitioner focuses on presenting symptoms, assumes that depression is like a physical illness and that the individual is sick. Thus problems which may be predominantly social or economic in origin may be wrongly identified as 'psychiatric disturbances' requiring physical treatments, such as drugs or ECT. This can encourage the acceptance of intolerable situations and legitimize and endorse the status quo. In this way the institution of medicine acts as an 'agency of disguised social control' (Roberts 1981, p. 14). Furthermore, the medical model assumes that people are passive sufferers of an illness, dependent upon an expert for a 'cure'. It restrains them from trying to understand their problems and finding ways of dealing with them themselves. Moreover, the patient–expert relationship is by definition characterised by inequality, where doctors have the power to 'define what is, and what is not, illness; what is, and what is not, appropriate behaviour in a patient; and what is to go on in the consulting room' (Roberts 1985 p.2). Doctors also determine what, if any, treatment is offered, as these women's experiences illustrate:

> The doctor said that I could be absolutely certain of a cure and never become ill again if I undertook the treatment. I was far too tearful and upset to take a rational view of this treat-ment — it was a leucotomy operation.

> I went to the psychiatrist feeling really ill with my depression and anxiety and badly wanted some kind of treatment. But he just said that I wasn't depressed only very unhappy and refused to treat me. That made me feel worse.

The power imbalance between doctor and patient may be particularly felt by women when doctors' decisions are based upon sex-stereotypical notions of appropriate behaviour. A now famous study by Broverman *et al* (1970) showed considerable sex-bias in the judgements of mental health clinicians. The clinicians were asked to choose from a list of characteristics those that would be typical of a 'mature, healthy, socially competent' man, woman or adult with sex unspecified. What was considered healthy for adults was also so for men, but not for women. Healthy women differed by being more submissive, passive, dependent, emotional, excitable, concerned with their appearance and so on. The study demonstrated that a double standard of mental health was operating in which women were placed in an impossible double bind of having to be both healthy adults and healthy females. Either their womanhood was questioned, or they were considered incompetent and immature. These findings have been largely replicated by later studies (Nowacki and Poe 1973; Fabrikant 1974; Aslin 1977).

Adherence to sex-stereotyped beliefs poses the potential problem that a clinician will view as psychopathological what is in fact only a marked deviation from traditional roles. Even when this does not occur, it is likely that both men and women will be encouraged to fit into prescribed roles, consequently inhibiting them from self-actualization and growth.

It is possible that in recent years, stereotyped beliefs may have softened slightly. Yet attitudes die hard, and sexism is still very much part of the value-base of our society. Indeed, doctors have not only been exposed to sex-role stereotyping through their own socialization, but also in some of the theories that they may have been taught. Freudian psychoanalytic theory with its astonishingly phallocentric and chauvinistic view of women is a case in point (see Freud 1925, 1931, 1933. See also works by Erikson 1963, 1968, and Lidz 1968 for blatant examples of sexism in psychoanalytic literature). Furthermore, the psychiatric profession is still male dominated. Thus, although progress may have been made in ridding the professions of more extreme forms of gender prejudice, subtle expressions of sexism are still likely to emerge.

The care and treatment offered by doctors does not always operate in the best interests of female patients. A depressed woman's feelings of inferiority, helplessness and low self-esteem may well be reinforced and perpetuated by the processes we have just outlined. Yet the medicalization of problems may at times serve the needs of women. For example, the guilt and sense of inadequacy that depressed women typically experience in feeling unable to fulfill social expectations may be assuaged by the identification of an illness. Such an explanation of their problems may reassure women and their families that there is indeed something wrong and that help is needed. Being defined as ill may be the only way that some women will feel allowed to stop and take care of themselves or have others take care of them. If this is doctor's orders so much the better! It is sometimes comforting to place trust in an expert and cease taking responsibilities.

Social workers need to be aware of these inherent contradictions in our medicalized world. They need to recognise the dangers of the medicalization process, but be prepared to use medical professionals wisely, when it serves the interests of their clients. Many women certainly seem disillusioned with the medical and psychiatric services, and feel that contact with them did more harm than good; however, others have had positive experiences. The women interviewed for this book generally spoke more sympathetically of psychiatrists who offered psychotherapy rather than drugs or ECT. Women were most likely to have received psychotherapy from the child psychiatric services. Many adult women spoke of the difficulty or impossibility of gaining psychotherapeutic help as an alternative, or even in addition to, physical therapies, either as an in- or out-patient.

I've been running a self-help group for seriously depressed people for a number of years and nobody in this area has ever been offered any psychotherapy at all. People who come to the group have seen psychiatrists who either give them more or different tablets and that's all.

I went to a psychiatrist at Child Guidance once a week. He was great, he just said 'tell me about it, tell me what it's like for you' and that's all I did. I cried a bit and he'd just say it was all right, and what I was feeling was fine ... it all started to make sense ... I got very different treatment a few years later from the adult services ... it was awful and I never want anything to do with the mental health services ever again...

The first doctor I saw was awful, he just gave me pills and didn't talk to me. But the second one (they change regularly), she was really nice. She used to treat me like I was human and not just a patient and come and chat and have tea with us on the ward. That was really good, but the other medical staff seemed to disapprove and said she was over-involved and she wasn't allowed to see me once I moved wards.

When I went to the doctor when I had my nervous breakdown — many years ago now — he just suggested I scrubbed and polished the floors ... I went to the psychiatrist at the hospital and he just gave me tablets but was unable to reassure me about the outcome of my breakdown — I didn't know if I'd ever be the same again ... When I saw another psychiatrist he told me I was just trying to shirk my responsibilities and this upset me so much I fainted at his feet.

My psychiatrist is really good, she listens, she accepts and she understands women!

After the abuse incident, I went to see a psychodynamic psychiatrist, but he was so removed from reality than when I tried to explain about the money situation he couldn't see that money could be a bar to me leaving. He was just so wrapped up in everybody's inner worlds rather than outer worlds it wasn't any good at all. Then we saw a behavioural psychologist for marital therapy and he was trying to get us to do things that would please the other partner, but I felt so negative towards him I didn't want to do anything that pleased him; so that was a washout as far as I was concerned.

Medical treatments for depression

Drugs

Women who go to their doctor for help with depression are most likely to be treated with medication. Women are the major recipients of psychotropic drugs and are more likely to be prescribed them than men presenting the same symptoms (Cooperstock and Lennard 1979; Jones *et al* 1984.) While there is certainly a growing number of doctors who are less ready to turn to the prescription pad, the use of pharmaco-therapy is still, on the whole, the treatment of choice for depression. Social workers need to have a good working knowledge of the drugs that are used, including their risks and side-effects, for clients may frequently call upon them to discuss their pill use: whether or not to take them, stay on them, change them, or come off them. Whilst doctors would obviously have to be involved in such decisions, the informed opinion of a social worker who can take time to discuss and explain things to her client is clearly of great value. Workers may also need to reassure clients that the symptoms they may be experiencing are due to the side-effects of the drugs, rather than an indication of another illness, since doctors do not always inform their patients of such worrying matters.

When I was in hospital I took a lot of Largactyl and anti-depressants. I couldn't focus properly and I thought I was going blind. I told the doctors and nurses about it, but they didn't say anything. I only learned later that it was a side-effect of the drugs.

Since the growing awareness of tranquillizer dependancy,

social workers may be increasingly involved in helping women to come off such drugs. For more information on tranquillizer withdrawal see Release (1982) and Melville (1984).

The following is a list of the most commonly prescribed drugs for 'uni-polar' depression:

Anti-depressants

Tricyclics. These are the most commonly prescribed anti-depressants and are generally used for treating moderate to severe depressions where there are also physical symptoms, such as appetite loss and sleep disturbance. They usually take three weeks or more to have an anti-depressant effect. Some tri-cyclics may also include a sedative used if people are also anxious and agitated. Large numbers of people get no relief at all from these drugs. Side-effects are a major problem, affecting at least one patient in five. The most common side-effects are: blurred vision, drowsiness, dry mouth, nausea, constipation, urine retention, sweating, weight gain, tremors, rashes, fuzzy thinking and dampening of sexual feelings. Elderly people tend to suffer most from these effects.

The following are the most commonly prescribed Tricyclics (brand names in brackets):

Imipramine   (Tofranil, Berkomine, Norpramine, Praminil)
Amitriptyline (Tryptizol, Lentizol, Domical, Suroten, Lim-
              bitrol, Triptafen)
Clomipranine (Anafranil)
Trimipramine (Surmontil)
Dothiepin   (Prothiaden)
Maprotiline   (Ludiomil)
Mianserin   (Bolvidon, Norval)

Mono-amine-oxidase inhibitors (MAOIS). These are prescribed less often than tricyclics because they are potentially dangerous when used in combination with certain drugs or foods (such as cheese, pickled fish, broad beans, yeast extracts and alcohol). They also take three or more weeks to take effect. Most common side-effects are dizziness or postural hypotension (faintness or dizziness with sudden changes in position). Less common are liver damage and psychotic episodes in those already susceptible to them, plus most of the side-effects associated with tricyclics.

The drugs most commonly prescribed in this group are (brand names in brackets);

Isucarboxazid	(Marplan)
Phenelzine	(Nardil)
Nialamid	(Niamid)

Anti-depressants are not considered to be addictive, although current research may prove otherwise.

Minor tranquillizers

Benzodiazepines. These are very commonly prescribed for 'reactive depression', indeed often overprescribed, with women going back year after year for repeat prescriptions. However, they will not help a depression directly; they are used principally to reduce any nervous tension or anxiety. Tranquillizers may take effect quickly (within an hour or two) but it is doubtful whether they are effective for periods beyond four months. Tranquillizers cause both physical and psychological dependence and sudden withdrawal may cause serious symptoms, such as increased anxiety and agitation, palpitations, insomnia, nausea, sweating, tension, appetite loss, headaches, feelings of unreality and reduced concentration and memory powers. Common side-effects include: constipation, confusion, headaches, rashes, nausea, drowsiness, dizziness, dry mouth, weight loss, lack of co-ordination and allergic reactions.

Tranquillizers have come under the government's limited drugs list, thus only the generic form of the drug can be obtained on the NHS. Those listed are: Chlordiazepoxide, Diazepam, Lorazepam and Oxazepam.

Hypnotics (sleeping pills). These are not usually very different from benzodiazepines; they are merely prescribed for the night rather than day. They tend not to have a sleep-inducing effect after a period of between three and twelve days, the user developing a tolerance to them, and often a dependency. They can inhibit dreaming and cause hangovers with drowsiness, dizziness, confusion, hypersensitivity and dry mouth. Confusion is often experienced soon after taking them, that is, before sleep, and can thus cause people to take extra doses, which may be dangerous.

Hypnotics on the NHS list are: Nitrazepam, Temazapam, and Triazolam.

Major tranquillizers

Phenothiazines: These are very strong drugs which are generally used for 'serious mental disorders'. They may be used in low doses for depressed people who are also very anxious or agitated. Side-effects may include: stiffness of neck and limbs, drowsiness and lethargy, weight gain, loss of sex drive and skin sensitivity to light. Long term use may cause serious damage to the central nervous system.

Commonly prescribed major tranquillizers are (brand names in brackets):

Chlorpromazine	(Largactyl, Chloractil, Dozine)
Flupenthixol	(Depixol)
Haliperidol	(Haldol, Seranace)
Perphenazine	(Fentazin)
Pimozide	(Orap)
Thioridazine	(Melleril)
Trifluoperazine	(Stelazine)

Minor tranquillizers may be useful to some people as a short-term emotional support to tide them over a crisis and anti-depressants may help to lift a depressed mood. Yet whilst psychotropic drugs can produce an initial reduction of symptoms, it has been suggested that a high proportion of drug users only improve symptomatically because of the placebo effect (Stanway 1981). Further, although there may be symptom relief, the social and interpersonal difficulties accompanying or causing the depression usually remain unchanged (Weissman and Paykel 1974) and relapse after the cessation of drug treatment is common. Bearing in mind these points and the potential risks and side-effects of the drugs, it is questionable whether the benefits of taking them outweigh the costs. A recent report (Prescott and Highley 1985) on the high risks of overdosing on psychotropic drugs concludes that tranquillizers (which, it notes, are more likely to be prescribed for depression than anti-depressants) may actually 'increase suicidal thoughts, *cause* depression and predispose to self-poisoning' (p.1633, my italics). It suggests that only a minority of patients prescribed these drugs 'have psychiatric illness for which drug treatment is indicated'. The majority have emotional and social problems for which 'there is no evidence that their regular use benefits ... On the contrary, these drugs may be positively harmful' (Prescott and Highley 1985, p.1635).

Taking pills which are seen as the answer to a problem, and suffering their side-effects, like fuzzy thinking and lethargy, are not likely to encourage people to explore what is wrong in their lives, and will almost certainly hamper their ability to change. Medication tends to suppress the natural coping mechanisms that come into play at a time of crisis and can, for example, interfere deleteriously with the normal process of grieving.

The over-prescribing of psychotropic drugs to women may be explained in terms of their ideological function (Roberts 1981; Penfold and Walker 1984). Pill-prescribing, like labelling someone as 'psychiatrically disturbed', individualizes social problems and thus maintains and legitimizes the oppressive conditions which contribute to women's 'sickness'. Women are dulled into accepting their predicament and are encouraged to adjust to the limitations of their roles. Doctors have been encouraged to use drugs in this way by advertisements from the pharmaceutical industries, which suggest that a single drug can cure any ill, social or emotional. Psychotropic drugs seem to have been sold on the basis that they can keep women coping with difficult child-care situations, housework, poor housing and so on.

Women may accept the drugs and diagnoses from doctors because they have been conditioned to look for the cause of problems within themselves, to revere and respect the judgement of 'experts' and to believe that there is indeed a 'pill for every ill'. Here are some women's views and experiences of taking drugs:

> I spent seven years dosed up on drugs — about half a dozen types — uppers, downers, put-you-to-sleepers, wake-you-uppers — I was a walking zombie. I was here in body but nothing else, I didn't know what was going on around me — if the house had burnt down I wouldn't have noticed it. I didn't realize it was due to the drugs till later, then I came off them and won't go on them again.

I've been on and off drugs — antidepressants, tranx, for many years — since I was 17. I think they help initially, maybe for a week or so, but then I think I'm only living to take another tablet. It doesn't solve anything, you still have to go back and face all the problems that were there before, but it perhaps helps you over a hump when life's really difficult and you can't handle it.

The doctor gave me some very strong tranquillizers to calm my nerves. So I was able to cope with work so I could earn enough to keep my six kids and pay the bills. But the pills made me very tired and drowsy.

The tablets made me really dizzy. I wouldn't have known if the baby had dropped on the floor or not, so I threw them out in the end.

I was on four different kinds of drugs, one lot to counteract the side effects of another. I'd been on two of them for years but suddenly the doctor decided I should come off them all. I stopped taking them for three days but had withdrawal symptoms. It was agony so they put me back on them again.

Tablets are like a crutch — they don't cure but they may relieve the problem a bit, and then they're worth taking. They can minimise the ill-effects of the depression.

Electroconvulsive therapy (ECT)
ECT is administered to people who are considered to have an endogenous depression and others who are severely depressed. It tends to be given after drug treatments have proved ineffective or when an immediate response is required, such as when there is a risk of suicide. Nowadays ECT is given with an anaesthetic and a muscle relaxant. The electric shock is then administered via two electrodes placed to the head, either with one on each side of the temples (bilateral ECT) or with both on the same side (unilateral ECT). Unilateral ECT is now generally favoured since it is considered to reduce the risks of memory disturbance. The procedure usually lasts a few moments and the patient is awake again within fifteen minutes. She may have a headache and suffer memory loss and confusion for an hour or so afterwards. Most people are given a course of

between five and twelve ECT treatments, at a rate of two to three a week.

ECT is generally considered by psychiatrists to be a very effective anti-depressant treatment, although no-one knows why or precisely how it works. However, the effects of ECT seem in most cases to be only short-lived and there are many patients who receive no relief at all from it. Furthermore, there is considerable debate as to whether ECT causes any permanent memory loss. Evidence both from research (Clare 1980) and subjective accounts are contradictory.

> I feel really angry about having had ECT because they didn't tell me it could give me memory damage, but it has. I can't remember a lot of my childhood, and if I don't look in my diary I can't remember things ...

> I didn't have any side-effects from ECT. It lifted my mood for a while but it didn't cure the depression.

Perhaps some people experience memory loss whilst others do not. It is certainly a risk that needs to be considered.

The extent to which ECT is used varies between hospitals. Anthony Clare considers that it is generally still a 'much abused and over-used method of treatment' (Clare 1980, p.266). For, he says, it is simpler for psychiatrists to recommend ECT than to engage in psychotherapy or to make a full investigation into a patient's situation. This often results in ECT being given to people with a 'reactive' (rather than 'endogenous') depression for which it has been found unhelpful. Social workers should therefore ensure that a full assessment is made of their client's problems and consider offering psychotherapy before ECT is tried, in addition to it, or as an alternative. Too frequently ECT is the sole method of treatment, yet it 'in no way militates against the simultaneous use of other treatment modalities' (Clare 1980, p.271).

The use of ECT requires consent from the individual or a second opinion in the case of patients who are detained under a six month section (Mental Health Act 1983 s.58). Social workers should consider discussing the viability of ECT with the medical team in both cases. In addition, they could discuss its use with patients and their families. It is also important that social workers ensure that people who are to have ECT are fully aware of the procedures of the operation. Not all psychiatrists undertake to inform patients about their treatments, and this only serves to increase anxiety.

Psychosurgery

Psychosurgery is a controversial form of treatment. It is a fairly rare but not extinct practice in Britain, carried out in only a few hospitals with special expertise in this area. Psychiatrists generally agree that it should only be used for depressed people who have a very severe and intractable condition, and undertaken only after other treatments have met with little or no success. Section 57 of the Mental Health Act 1983 states that psychosurgery can only be given with the consent of the patient *and* a second opinion. In addition, a panel appointed by the Mental Health Act Commission must agree that the consent is valid, and the doctor on the panel must certify in writing that the treatment is necessary. Necessity is determined by the doctor fulfilling his legal duty to consult two other people who have been caring for the patient — one a nurse and one neither a nurse nor a doctor.

Those social workers working with the Commission, or in the hospitals in which psychosurgery is undertaken, are likely to be involved in discussions and decisions on the advisability of this treatment. In these cases workers should have a specialist knowledge of the subject, be informed about the various types of operations and be aware of any recent evaluation or outcome studies. As yet there have been no controlled clinical trials on psychosurgery. This form of treatment, which is necessarily drastic and irreversible, thus continues to be of uncertain value and remains ethically controversial.

Hospitalisation

Each year many thousands of women are admitted to psychiatric hospitals with depression. Indeed, more psychiatric hospital beds are occupied by people suffering from depression than from any other condition. The experience of hospitalisation will clearly be different for each woman, but it is generally one that makes a deep and lasting impression. For some, hospitalisation can mean a much needed break from the strains and stresses of daily life, an opportunity not to be responsible, a chance to think and talk over problems. It may also offer a place and time when women can feel that they are being taken care of and provided with the rest and treatment that they need. But for many women hospitalisation affords few of these benefits. Instead it can be a degrading and frightening experience which brings only more problems: problems of institutionalisation, stigmatisation, boredom, isolation, and often, deeper depression. In danger of being infantilised, victimised or abused, women may become more helpless and desperate. Often they will be offered no more than drugs, ECT and occupational therapy for treatment. Here are some extracts from women talking about their often mixed experiences in psychiatric hospitals and the effects they have had on them:

I went into hospital as a voluntary patient, even though it broke my heart to do so. I thought 'my God, I'm not mad' and I sobbed and sobbed all the way there ... I refused to take drugs, I didn't want any at all. I was able to talk there to a young woman doctor and to some of the nurses. I just needed someone to talk through things with, to help me to sort my own mind out, 'cause I was so mixed up ... through talking I pulled out of it, and I could feel my confidence coming back ... I agreed with my doctor that I would go into town to look at this flat I could rent ... When I got back to the hospital I was called into the nurse's office to find a stern looking doctor I'd never seen before. She said I'd been out without permission and asked why I'd run away. I told her my doctor knew where I was, that I had permission etc., but she had forgotten to tell the ward sister and had gone off duty. They refused to ring up and check, and decided to believe my husband who had phoned whilst I was out and told them I'd run away and had been causing trouble. The doctor — a consultant — decided she wanted me locked up and that was that, she didn't want any explanations from me. I was put in the most dangerous ward of the hospital — it was for violent mental patients who were to be under lock and key at all times ... I cried all night in this locked ward, petrified of the other patients. I sat on this chair afraid to move — the patients were tearing each other apart. The next morning my own doctor came and stuck up for me. The consultant thought I ought to stay in the locked ward ... but then they got another consultant who agreed that I shouldn't be in there and got me out, back to my own ward ...

I went to B hospital for three weeks. I hated every minute of it. They put you in a room and let you get on with it. You see a psychiatrist every now and then ... he just gave me more pills, there was no counselling or anything. When I left three weeks later I felt worse than when I went in ... They never tell you anything about what's going on — like why I had to have a blood test and that, and I think that's what made me feel worse ...

In hospital they wouldn't let me take my son out on my own — for the whole six weeks I was there. A couple of times I tried, but they stopped me ... I didn't know if I was a voluntary patient or not, I might have been under a section. It felt like it 'cause I wasn't allowed out, but they didn't say ...

The night staff treated us like children — we all had to be in bed by 10.30 pm and take our pills at 10 pm. They wanted us to be adults in the day, to look after our children, but at night they treated us like children. So, sometimes we acted like children — played stupid games and giggled. One nurse sometimes got really cross and one time she made us all go to bed at 10pm ... They always sedated us at night if they could, so things would be easier on the ward.

I hated going into hospital so I rebelled against everything and ran away. I felt I was being trapped, that I was being kept imprisoned there. Even though I was a voluntary patient I just felt they were going to keep me there and I didn't have any control over anything ... After a few weeks in hospital though, I felt safe and I didn't want to go home — I'd gone the other way. They'd taken away the problems and I didn't have any responsibility for anything. So I was afraid to go home, to be on my own again ...

When I was in hospital I felt even worse than before when I worked and had things to take my mind off how awful everything was. But in hospital I just spent the whole day brooding about how dreadful everything was ... I looked around me and because I was with people who'd been in hospital a long time and looked worse than I did, they scared me and I thought I'd end up like them and that freaked me out, I thought I'd rather be dead than that. It got worse and I got more and more unhappy and I took an overdose and then they sectioned me ...

In hospital there weren't enough nurses, they were always busy so you couldn't really ask them to stop and talk with you. Sometimes they stopped to talk to you, but then they had to rush off so you never got the attention you needed. Even when I was specialled — that's when a nurse is with you all the time — I was getting a lot of attention, but it was very negative and they hated it. When you know someone's watching you all the time it makes you want to run away even more, so if you get a second to yourself, you're off. It was just counter-productive.

The second time I went into hospital they treated me more as a person because they knew me and they were nicer to me. I felt more responsible and they trusted me more. I was afraid of killing myself and I didn't want to, but thought I might ... so hospital was like a protection.

The doctors make you feel that as a patient you're not quite as good as everyone else ... you're always just another patient and no-one is allowed to become involved with you, if they do, they're told they're over-involved and taken in and you're moved or they're moved. It makes you feel you're not quite worthy of having friends.

I saw the psychiatrist the morning after I'd taken the overdose. He was horrible ... he just said what a selfish thing it was to do to try and kill myself and when was I going to get on with my life and stop blaming other people for it? He just blamed me for everything that was happening without listening to me.

People treat you differently if they know you've been in a psychiatric hospital. They don't want to take the time to get to know you because they're scared and worried you'll go mad on them.

Women in hospitals are often at the mercy of sexist attitudes held by doctors and nurses. For example, women may be encouraged to take on traditional female roles and behaviour, such as caring for other patients and spending more time on their appearance. They may only be deemed 'healthy' once they have adopted such roles:

> The nurses used to say things like 'oh doesn't she look well' just because she'd got her make-up on.

> They wanted me to go and work on the geriatric ward because they knew I'd worked in one before. I didn't want to but they pressurised me, I think because they thought that as a woman I should be caring for people. On each ward there's a helper and nearly all of them are women.

Women from ethnic minorities may suffer the stresses of racism as well as sexism. A hospital experience is likely to be particularly stressful for those who have different languages, diets, customs and habits, from those prevalent in the institution. Apart from the problems of misdiagnosis and misinterpretation of behaviour already mentioned, patients who do not speak English may well be denied access to any kind of talking therapy in favour of drugs and/or ECT (Francis 1984).

District social workers, whether 'approved' or not, need to be aware of the type of psychiatric hospitals in their area and the kinds of treatments that are on offer. But before considering admission into a hospital of whatever kind, social workers should examine all alternatives to it. This is as essential for voluntary as for compulsory admissions, where the Mental Health Act 1983 now requires a search for alternatives. The voluntary sector, including women's organisations, is producing an increasing number of mental health facilities. However, given the demand, and despite policies of community care, these are few and far between in most areas. In the final analysis social workers may have little choice but to recommend hospital to depressed women who are so withdrawn that they cannot cope with life at all, to those who are at serious risk of suicide or self-injury, or to those who need a respite from stress and responsibilities.

When admission to hospital is necessary, social workers will need to remember that such an event may cause a crisis for a woman as well as her family. In order to effect the move with the minimum of distress, workers could begin by eliciting the views, fears and anxieties of all concerned. Fears of the unknown may sometimes be allayed simply by providing information about such matters as hospital procedures and routines, visiting hours and what can be expected in terms of treatment. The depressed woman and other family members may need to be reassured that the family will be able to cope without their wife/mother/daughter and that support from the SSD or elsewhere will be forthcoming if necessary. Fears about family disintegration can be allayed if channels of communication between a woman and her family are kept open from the beginning and are maintained whilst she is in hospital. The risks of difficulties arising on return from hospital may also be minimised by this means. In addition, social workers may need to make arrangements for the care of children or elderly dependents and deal with a number of practical matters, such as social security benefits, the payment of rent and bills and informing friends and relatives. All such matters are likely to be a cause of concern and anxiety and social workers can help by anticipating them and knowing how to deal with them efficiently.

Once a woman has been admitted to hospital, social workers, whether from the district or the hospital, may take on a number of different roles for the benefit of their clients: a mediatory role between patient and doctors and/or between the client and the outside world, a therapeutic role and an advocative one. Close cooperation between community and hospital social workers will be necessary. Social workers might also consider adopting an adversarial role. Instead of limiting their tasks to those which the doctors have deemed appropriate for them, they might take an active part in challenging some of the assumptions and attitudes of the medical professionals and the practices that are carried out on a daily basis within psychiatric institutions. In addition, feminist and other like minded workers could provide an impetus for change within the system by, for example, forming groups for the purpose of consciousness raising, campaigning and support. The work of such a group might include holding and giving talks and seminars on matters such as women's psychology, feminist therapy, or sexism and psychiatry. It might also include pressing for more psychotherapeutic and counselling work, or for a language interpreting service and alternative meals for people from ethnic minorities. Feminist social workers could also be instrumental in encouraging and helping patients to set up their own groups, unions or councils. By such means the users and ex-users of the service can be afforded the opportunity to feed back their experiences and opinions to professionals and policy-makers, campaign on specific issues on their own behalf, and hopefully, have a voice in the future planning of resources. The growing dissatisfaction of current hospital practices and treatments needs to be harnessed and turned into positive action for the benefit of all patients.

Summary
In this chapter we have looked at the role of social work with depressed women, particularly as it interacts with medicine and psychiatry. In doing so we have considered depression from a clinical point of view, as well as from the perspective of women's own experiences. We have seen that medical professionals can have something of value to offer female clients, but that often their care and treatments do not function in the best interests of women. Doctors and psychiatrists may not address the psychosocial and socio-structural factors that so frequently contribute to women's depression and may offer treatments that are deleterious and inexpedient. By pathologising women's problems, doctors are in danger of reinforcing women's feelings of depression as well as perpetuating and legitimizing the adverse social conditions from which women need to escape to improve their mental health. It has been suggested therefore, that social workers take a prominent role in dealing with depressed women and that they challenge the medicalization process where necessary.

Further reading
Brown, G.W. and Harris, T. (1978) *Social Origins of Depression*, London: Tavistock Publications.

Butler, A. and Pritchard, C. (1983) *Social Work and Mental Illness*, London: Macmillan.

Clare, A. (1980) *Psychiatry in Dissent*, London: Tavistock Publications.

Dominian, J. (1976) *Depression*, London: Fontana.

Howell, E. and Bayes, M. (eds) (1981) *Women and Mental Health*, New York: Basic Books.

Hudson, B.L. (1982) *Social Work with Psychiatric Patients*, London: Macmillan.

Levine, S.V., Kamin, L.E. and Levine, E.L. (1974) 'Sexism

and Psychiatry', *American Journal of Orthopsychiatry*, 44, 3, 327–36.

Littlewood, R. and Lipsedge, M. (1982) *Aliens and Alienists*, Harmondsworth: Penguin.

Melville, J. (1984a) *The Tranquillizer Trap and How to Get Out of It*, Glasgow: Fontana.

Melville, J. (1984b) *First Aid in Mental Health*, London: Unwin Paperbacks.

Nairne, K. and Smith, G. (1984) *Dealing with Depression*, London: The Women's Press.

Olsen, M.R. (ed.) (1984) *Social Work and Mental Health. A Guide for the Approved Social Worker*, London and New York: Tavistock Publications.

Penfold, P.S. and Walker, G.A. (1984) *Women and the Psychiatric Paradox*, Milton Keynes: Open University Press.

Rack, P. (1982) *Race, Culture and Mental Disorder*, London: Tavistock Publications.

Stanway, A. (1981) *Overcoming Depression*, Feltham: Hamlyn.

Some biographies and novels give excellent insights into women's experiences of depression and/or hospitalisation:

Arden, N. (1977) *Child of a System*, London: Quartet Books.

De Beauvoir, S. (1984) *The Woman Destroyed*, London: Flamingo/Fontana.

Frame, J. (1980) *Faces in the Water*, London: The Women's Press.

Gordon, B. (1980) *I'm Dancing as Fast as I Can*, London: Bantam Books.

Perkins Gilman, C. (1981) *The Yellow Wallpaper*, London: Virago Press.

Plath, S. (1966) *The Bell Jar*, London: Faber & Faber.

2 Causes and Explanations for Depression in Women

There is a general consensus in the psychological literature that women exceed men in the rate of depression. In General Practice, hospital and community surveys, women of all ages have been found to suffer in this respect more than men (Dohrenwend and Dohrenwend 1976; Weissman and Klerman 1977; Radloff 1980). However, there has been some debate as to whether these findings reflect a 'true' prevalence or merely a methodological artifact. It has been suggested that the different rates of depression may be attributed to women's greater willingness to admit affective symptoms, or to the higher frequency with which they seek medical help. Another theory advanced is that the incidence of depression is equally divided between the sexes but that men and women express it differently. It is suggested that men turn to alcohol or crime and consequently preponderate in the alcoholism and criminal statistics rather than the mental health statistics. In a detailed review of the research, however, Weissman and Klerman (1977) found the 'artifact hypothesis' to be unsubstantiated. For, first, although women may acknowledge their distress more frequently than men, it does not appear to be because they find it less stigmatising or more worthy of approval. Second, explaining the fact that women seek treatment for depression more often than men in terms of sex differences in the utilization of medical services, does not account for the preponderance of depressed women in community surveys. Finally, it is debatable whether men who turn to alcohol, violence or crime are actually depressed. It may be interesting to speculate on the point, but as yet there is no concrete evidence to support this hypothesis. Thus there seem to be sufficient grounds for concluding that the female preponderance in depression is real and not an artifact. We shall now examine possible explanations for this finding.

Genetic and hormonal explanations for depression in women

The differential rate of depression between the sexes is commonly attributed to biological factors — to an hereditary predisposition or to the female endocrine system. Evidence to support the view that there is a genetic factor operating in depression is, however, meagre and what evidence there is does not adequately explain the sex differences. In addition, the pattern of the relationship of hormone levels to depression is inconsistent. The post-natal period certainly seems to contribute to increasing rates of depression. Premenstrual tension and oral contraception also have this effect, but only to a very small degree. However, contrary to widely held views, there is good evidence that the menopause has little or no effect in increasing rates of depression, and pregnancy significantly decreases the risks. It seems that we can conclude, as Weissman and Klerman (1977) do, that whilst a proportion of the sex differences in depression, particularly in the child-bearing years, can be explained by reference to women's hormones, this factor is not sufficient in itself to account for such a large differential. More convincing explanations for the differential rates of depression seem to be in social and psychosocial factors.

Social and psychosocial explanations for women's depression

Conventional theories about the causes and nature of depression do not on the whole address themselves to women's specific vulnerability to this problem. Nevertheless, they provide a useful framework in which to explore the subject. Interestingly, these theories do seem to attribute depression to factors which are especially likely to pertain to women, given their current roles and status in society. We shall now examine some of the most influential theories and briefly indicate their implications for women's susceptibility to depression. A more comprehensive analysis of women's vulnerability will be offered in Chapter 3.

Psychoanalytic theories

Freud (1917) considered depression to be a pathological reaction to a loss, in which angry impulses are turned inward against the self. In brief, Freud argued that an over-involvement and ambivalence between the ego and a lost love object leads to difficulties in reconciling or resolving the loss. In such cases, object loss becomes ego loss, resulting in a lowering of self-regard and esteem; the ambivalence in the relationship between ego and object is transformed into intra-psychic conflict.

Other psychoanalytic writers, whilst offering variants of Freud's theory, essentially concur that loss, either real or imagined, is the major cause of depression, and that depressed people tend to form very dependent and ambivalent relationships, suffer from excessive guilt and low self-esteem and introject hostility (Abraham 1911; Rado 1928). Another important element of the psychoanalytic approach is that early childhood experiences, particularly deprivation and distorted parental relationships, can sensitize adults to depression (Klein 1935; Bowlby 1969, 1980).

Women's lives and roles are often full of changes which make them susceptible to loss. Because they are socialized to be 'other-orientated', women tend to place an immense investment into personal relationships, which makes them 'more vulnerable to the stresses of deprivation of such ties, and hence depression' (Bernard 1976, p.228). The socialization and childhood experiences of girls, who are often less valued than boys, also tends to predispose women to depression later in life. Females frequently develop only a rather fragile sense of self and a meagre concept of their own personal worth and identity. Consequently, they tend to be dependent on others for their self-definition, and for approval and support. Women are often emotionally as well as economically dependent on men. This may well result in their experiencing greater ambivalence in their close personal relationships. Furthermore, the female role militates against open expressions of hostility and anger, giving women less opportunity to act out their disappointments.

Bibring, a later psychoanalytic writer, takes a somewhat different line from the aforementioned psychoanalysts. He considers depression to be caused by frustration in achieving success, rather than the loss of a loved object. Depression results when a longing to be valued and esteemed is met by a realisation that these goals are unobtainable; it is the result of 'the ego's shocking awareness of its helplessness in regard to its aspirations' (Bibring, 1953). This theory has particular significance for contemporary women; for potential access to new opportunities has led to higher expectations, which are nevertheless frustrated for the many women who have to remain in traditional roles.

Behavioural theories

Behaviourists such as Lazarus (1968, 1976) and Lewinsohn (1974) essentially consider depression to be a consequence of a reduction of positive reinforcements in a person's life. An insufficiency of reinforcers may be induced by environmental change (such as the death of a loved one) or a deficit in social skills. As we shall see in Chapter 3, women's roles are often unsatisfying and lacking in positive reinforcement. Many women find it difficult to elicit positive reinforcers because they have been encouraged to be passive rather than assertive. They may have learned to depend on covert or manipulative behaviour, rather than on open and direct communication, to achieve desired aims. Such strategies tend to be detrimental to women's personal relationships and are ineffective in the long term.

Another behavioural theory of depression is that of *learned helplessness* (Seligman 1975). Seligman conducted laboratory experiments in which he found that animals, and later humans who were repeatedly subject to unpleasant stimuli outside of their control learned that they were helpless. This meant that in later tests they remained passive and did not even attempt to gain control over circumstances. This learned helplessness is induced when individuals believe that an outcome is independent of their response, that is, that they have no control over it. Seligman found parallels between this state of helplessness and reactive depression. He argued that people who are denied the opportunity to control their environment in their early years are more likely to react with learned helplessness in adult life.

Seligman's studies stimulated considerable interest as well as criticism. In response to the criticism and in an attempt to compensate for some theoretical weaknesses, Seligman and his colleagues introduced a cognitive component into the theory (Abramson *et al* 1978). They postulated that depression occurred when people *perceived* themselves negatively as a result of experiencing helplessness. Those particularly prone to depression, the theory states, view their problems in terms of long-standing personal inadequacies, rather than as a result of specific situations which are likely to be short-lived.

Seligman's theory may highlight some of the reasons why women are more prone to depression than men. Girls are generally socialized to be passive, helpless and dependent. They 'are taught that their personal worth and survival depends not on effective responding to life's situations but on physical beauty and appeal to men, i.e. that they have no direct control over the circumstances of their lives.' (Beck and Greenberg 1974, p.120). Women have few opportunities for reversing this tendency later in life since they typically assume powerless roles. Furthermore, women seem to be socialized to have a 'negative attributional style'. Studies have shown, for example, that women are more likely than men to attribute their success to luck or other external factors, and their failures to personal inadequacies. They are less likely to expect to succeed in the future and consequently less likely to try (Mednick, Tangri and Hoffman 1975).

Cognitive theories

Cognitive theory (Beck 1976) also postulates a relationship between perceptions and depression. Here cognitions (thoughts) have a primary causal role. Human emotions are seen as a result of what people think or tell themselves. Depression, specifically, is caused by negative perceptions of oneself, the world and the future. A depressive episode may be externally precipitated, by a loss for example, but it is the individual's perception and appraisal of the event that renders it depression-inducing. Beck suggests that the depressive's negative view of life derives from 'early experiences' such as loss of a parent in childhood. He also suggests that the prevalence of depression in women might be explained by the fact that women 'tend to see themselves as needfully dependent, helpless, repressed.' Women may be 'more definitively bound by internalised cultural expectations than by specific obstacles to their happiness and success.' (Beck and Greenberg 1974, p.120). Such 'internalized oppression' certainly contributes to women's vulnerability to depression. However, for many women, particularly working-class and black women, there are many obstacles to success that are located in structural conditions and not just the thoughts inside their heads. In areas of education, employment and social security, for example, women are quite clearly still discriminated against. Nevertheless, if internal obstacles could be overcome, women might indeed get more out of life.

None of these psychological theories are sufficient in

themselves to explain depression, or women's particular vulnerability to it. The principal deficiencies in the theories we have discussed may be summarised as follows: psychoanalytic perspectives give insufficient weight to the depressed person's current life-circumstances; behavioural theories fail to take into account how feelings and past experiences influence behaviour, and also ignore the importance of thoughts as mediators of behaviour; the 'learned helplessness' model does not suggest which sorts of experiences of uncontrollability are particularly likely to result in depression; and finally, all these theories totally ignore the socio-structural context in which depressed people are placed. It is left to sociological research to offer some insights in this respect.

A sociological perspective

Brown and Harris (in Brown *et al* 1975, and Brown and Harris 1978) have carried out one of the most influential sociological studies of depression. They conducted a survey of approximately 500 women in an inner London suburb to examine the influence of social factors on the development of depression. They found that 15 per cent of their sample were suffering from a 'definitive affective disorder', whilst 18 per cent were borderline cases. Thus 33 per cent of the women interviewed were experiencing some degree of depression. In 83 per cent of cases traumatic life events or major ongoing difficulties preceded the onset of depression. Most of these traumatic events or 'provoking agents' involved the experience of loss or disappointment concerning either a person, object, role or idea. Ongoing difficulties included bad housing and unsatisfactory marriages. Brown and Harris also identified four 'vulnerability factors' which increased the likelihood of women becoming depressed when faced with such stresses. These were: three or more children under fourteen living at home; lack of an intimate or confiding relationship; loss of mother in childhood; and lack of employment outside the home. These factors contributed to women's sense of low self-esteem and impotence, making them vulnerable to the effects of loss and stress.

Brown and Harris (1978 and Brown *et al* 1975) found that working-class women were five times more likely to become depressed than middle-class women because of their greater likelihood of experiencing the first three 'vulnerability factors' just mentioned. However, the women's class position was determined by that of their husbands', whether present or absent, which may have distorted the results slightly. The crucial variable in this context may be one often correlated with class, that is, the income (or lack of it) available to the woman, rather than class status itself. The association between poverty or 'economic strain' and depression has been corroborated by other research (Pearlin and Johnson 1977).

Other studies also lend weight to the view that women's particular vulnerability to depression lies predominantly in social factors. Gove and Tudor (1973), for example, found that higher overall rates of mental illness were largely accounted for by married women. They attribute this to the restrictive roles of married women who remain at home and to the frustrating nature of housework. Rosenfield's study (1980) supports this. She found that when wives were not working and when the division of labour in the home was organised on traditional lines, women had much higher levels of depression than men. However, the sex differences in rates of depression seemed to reverse when both partners fulfulled less traditional roles, and when the wife worked outside the home.

The existence of a significant link between 'clinical' depression and women's social circumstances and life experiences has been convincingly demonstrated by the sociological research discussed above. Brown and Harris (1978) note that their findings apply to all types of depression, including psychotic forms, although they suggest that 'there was a slight hint that a sub-group of depression might exist that was without a provoking agent.' The significance of social factors in depression has important implications for the role of social workers in dealing with women who are depressed.

Summary
This chapter has looked at a number of different theories in an attempt to explain women's vulnerability to depression. Social and psychosocial perspectives together present useful insights into the problem. The theories seem to suggest that women who have internalized societal prescriptions of female behaviour and those who fulfil stereotypically female roles are especially vulnerable to depression. This vulnerability is likely to be increased by adverse social circumstances. In the next chapter we shall look in more detail at what makes women depressed.

Further reading

Blaney, P.H. (1977) 'Contemporary Theories of Depression: Critique and Comparison,' *Journal of Abnormal Psychology*, 86, 3, 203–23.

Brown, G.W. and Harris, T. (1978) *Social Origins of Depression*, London: Tavistock Publications.

Dohrenwend, B.P. and Dohrenwend, B.S. (1976) 'Sex Differences and Psychiatric Disorders,' *American Journal of Sociology*, 81, 6, 1447–54.

Freud, S. (1917) Mourning and Melancholia, *Standard Edn*, vol. 14 (1957) London: Hogarth Press. Reprinted in *On Metapsychology. The Theory of Psychoanalysis* (1984), Harmondsworth: Penguin.

Gove, W.R. and Tudor, J.F. (1973) 'Adult Sex Roles and Mental Illness,' *American Journal of Sociology*, 78, 812–35.

Lazarus, A.A. (1968) 'Learning Theory and the Treatment of Depression', *Behaviour Research and Therapy*, 6, 83–9.

Seligman, M.E.P. (1975) *Helplessness*, San Francisco: Freeman.

Weissman, M.M. and Klerman, G.L. (1977) 'Sex Differences in the Epidemiology of Depression,' *Archives of General Psychiatry*, 34, 98–111.

3 Depression in the Lives of Women – a Feminist Perspective

The purpose of this chapter is to alert social workers to some of the influences, processes and events in the lives of women that may play a part in making them depressed. Inevitably, we have not given a detailed and comprehensive account of every aspect in women's lives which may make them depressed. We have merely highlighted some of the most crucial times and experiences, focusing on issues that *particularly* affect women. In doing so connections are made between personal and social or political factors, between external oppression and depression. We shall see not only how adverse circumstances may themselves cause depression, but also how the external oppression of women reared in a patriarchal society and socialized to be second-class citizens can be internalised and converted into self-oppression. Internal and external oppression operate in a dynamic relationship maintaining women in a powerless, inferior and sometimes, depressed position. Sexism, however, is only one form of oppression; there are many others, such as those relating to class, race, age, sexual orientation and so on. Some of these will be discussed, for every further dimension of oppression imposes additional strains and stresses which may serve to increase women's vulnerability to depression.

Common themes and issues concerning women's lives, at various stages and in many situations, emerge throughout this chapter. For example, we see how women are often in a position of being dependent on others, or having others dependent on them. They are typically vulnerable to loss and low self-esteem, and frequently their depressions are associated with failing to live up to unrealistic and contradictory expectations imposed upon them by others. Women's depressions are also often connected with their powerlessness in the external world.

We shall now turn to examine some aspects of women's socialization which may account for their particular susceptibility to depression. Various issues and problems in women's lives which may induce a depressive episode are then discussed.

Socialization into the female role

The experiences of the early years can be crucial for developing inner resources and strengths, making individuals more or less vulnerable to depression. While not denying the importance of current circumstances in contributing to depression, we shall examine here how early experiences and socialization patterns can affect women's functioning and vulnerability in later life.

All human beings have certain basic emotional needs — the need for love, nurture, understanding, acceptance, approval and so on. Those who are deprived of these essentials are liable to feel vulnerable and needy, and to be left with a dearth of inner resources to cope with life's demands. Without positive early experiences it may also be difficult to form successful, emotionally gratifying relationships in adulthood. Those who have never been loved may find it hard to love others, and to be loved and lovable themselves. They may unconsciously invite rejection and disapproval as confirmation of their own feelings of worthlessness and unworthiness. Nevertheless, further rejection and failure to have their needs met may well reawaken past feelings of deprivation and lead to an episode of depression. Some research on the relationship between early and later life experiences has found that a loss in adult life is more likely to induce a severe depression if a person has suffered a childhood loss — either in the form of actual separation or emotional absence (White 1977; Brown and Harris 1978).

Many women explain their depressions, especially those that the professionals label as 'endogenous', by reference to childhood experiences:

> I think it was my childhood that caused my depression. I lost my mother when I was under a year old and my father remarried three years later. My stepmother was like the ones in the storybooks. She treated me and my brother very badly. She used to beat us and not allow us food as punishment ... she wouldn't let us go out to play or listen to music. We had to work in the house, but she did nothing, she just used us as cleaners, from when I was about six or seven she used to abuse me in every possible way — physically and mentally.

> I was never a happy child. As a child I always felt I was unwanted. There was never any physical contact and I didn't come from a family where feelings were shown, so through-

out my life I always had to keep things in, to repress feelings to fit in with the family ... I feel very unnurtured because I lacked physical comfort and attention. ... As a child I had terrible nightmares where my mother was trying to get rid of me, or someone took my mother from me. I didn't know if my mother cared or not but basically she was never there for me ... I realise I wasn't validated as a person, I wasn't allowed to be what I was ... My unhappy childhood gave me a very negative view of myself ... I think that's the cause of my 'endogenous' depressions.

I had a terrible upbringing. My mother and father couldn't manage to look after us when we were young and we had to go to work at ten years old — this was in Jamaica ... We had to work to survive and buy food. My parents gave us away one by one to different people — black people, because they couldn't afford to keep us. I had to work for these people, do shopping and housework and things and they didn't send me to school, so I never learnt to read. It's very difficult not being able to read — some people think you're stupid if they know.

Let us look for a moment at why females may be more prone to unsatisfactory early relationships than males. What in their early years might make them more vulnerable to depression later in life?

Many baby girls start life as a minor, or even major disappointment to their parents who would have preferred a baby boy (Belotti 1975). This start to life as a 'second best' is frequently carried into childhood and adolescence. For instance, boys are still often given greater encouragement for educational and other personal achievements. Female children may thus begin to feel that they are not intended to be so important in the external world:

I was brought up to believe I was worthless. The girls in the family were told that the boys were better than us, they needed all the education and our role in life is just to get married, have kids and look after a home.

Such feelings of inferiority and insignificance may be reinforced by other aspects of a girl's socialization. Little girls are expected to grow up like their own mothers, to develop a keen sense of the needs of others and to place those needs before their own. From early on they learn to please, to comply and give others what they want and expect. By watching and identifying with their mothers they learn that to be loved and approved of they must be nurturant and emotionally giving (Eichenbaum and Orbach 1982). This means that as women they either have little sense of what their own needs are, or they feel that their needs are unimportant and unworthy of being attended to. They may carry with them a vague sense of deprivation, and a feeling that something is missing inside them. These feelings may not always be recognised for what they are, but instead may be expressed in terms of the symptoms of depression.

Feelings of deprivation may also be experienced by women who as girls were not nurtured sufficiently or not given enough physical affection:

> There was never any physical contact in my family. I don't remember ever having any cuddles. I was just not a picked up, held child ... My own personal needs were very strongly that I needed that physical contact but that I never got it.

Research studies (Moss 1970; Maccoby and Jacklin 1974; Belotti 1975) have shown that for various reasons little girls do not get as much physical attention and affection as little boys. Girls who have been deprived in this way may later find it difficult to have emotionally gratifying sexual relationships.

Girls who are brought up in families with traditional sex-role expectations may be deprived in another way. They will be taught, first and foremost, to be clean and tidy, pretty and passive, coy and attentive to others, to stay close to the home and not to take risks in the 'dangerous world'. They may not be allowed to develop another side of themselves — a strong, independent, adventurous, assertive side. Thus as adults they may have a tendency to be passive, dependent, fearful, submissive and self-sacrificing. Such characteristics often form the core components of depression and would thus not appear to be conducive to good mental health. Indeed, research by Bem (1974, 1975) showed that a high degree of sex-stereotyped behaviour in women correlated with high levels of anxiety, low self-esteem and generally poor emotional adjustment. In contrast, women with an androgynous identity (i.e. with both 'masculine' and 'feminine' characteristics) were found to be more outgoing, creative and successful professionally. This suggests that women pay a high price for maintaining traditional feminine behaviour and roles and that those with an androgynous identity are likely to be more protected against depression.

Whilst current social trends are tending to allow women greater flexibility in their life-styles and behaviour, there are still many who continue to live, and to bring up their children, according to restrictive sex-stereotypical codes. Indeed, women and girls are still presented with only a rather narrow range of images with which to identify. For example, the educational system, books, the media, all serve to perpetuate and reinforce similar views about how females should be and behave. The most typical images are of young, white women who are beautiful sex-objects for men's desire, or women who are sexless maternal beings whose sole role is to act as servicer and provider to men and children. Such images encourage women to live up to ideals that are unrealizable and undesirable; they suggest that those who do not are failures. Failing to meet such ideals can be a depressing experience. Many women live with enduring feelings of self-doubt and self-deprecation because they do not conform to what is supposed to be the norm for them.

In conclusion we can see that women may be vulnerable to depression because (a) they may have been socialized to take on inferior and subordinate roles and hence may have a fragile sense of their own worth and power; (b) the feminine characteristics and roles they may have been required to adopt from childhood onwards offer only a limited range of actions and adaptive resources, making them vulnerable in times of stress; and (c) they are usually encouraged to aspire to false goals, expectations and images which have been defined for them by others (i.e. men) and are rarely entirely realizeable.

Life-stages

This section explores some of the potentially depression-inducing strains and stresses that may arise for women during certain life-stages. Whilst not wishing to underplay the continuity of life experience, we have nevertheless chosen to highlight certain issues and problems that are most likely to occur, or become important, at particular times in a woman's life.

Adolescence

Adolescence in this society tends to be characterised by intense
and volatile emotions and swings of mood, by uncertainties and
instabilities. Adults may mistake the symptoms of depression
for these 'normal' processes of adolescence. Negotiating the
transition from childhoold to adulthood can be fraught with difficulties, and it may not take much to tip the balance from being
'normally' worried and low to feeling intensely depressed and
suicidal.

Common problems during adolescence include: relationship
difficulties with parents, peers and sexual partners; difficulties
at school associated with success, failure or exams; unwanted
pregnancies; unemployment; and loneliness and isolation.
Research has shown that female adolescents are particularly
likely to experience these factors as stressful (Burke and Weir
1978), and hence they are most likely to be depressed by them.

Concerns beginning in adolescence, such as those to do with
identity formation, body-image and sexuality may be especially
difficult for young women. We saw earlier how women's views
of themselves are so much affected by images of what they
should be. Adolescent women may be particularly vulnerable to
the injunctions of the media and become preoccupied with their
personal appearance. For many, adolescence heralds a
beginning of their dislike of their own bodies, of shame and embarrassment about their developing breasts, pubic hairs, hips,
stomachs and so on. Negative attitudes towards menstruation
still abound, so that for many girls, starting their periods can
also be an embarrassing, anxiety-provoking experience. For
some young women the reality of these bodily changes are too
much to cope with. They may attempt to control them, even
deny them, for example by dieting or bingeing, sometimes to
the point of anorexia, or bulimia. Depression is often a con-
comitant of such eating disorders.

The physical changes of adolescence are associated with
sexual and identity development. A woman's developing
sexuality often induces adult/parental warnings and restrictions. Whilst boys are often encouraged to experiment sexually,
girls are warned of being promiscuous and getting pregnant.
They may even be considered to be in 'moral danger', which
may lead to the imposition of a care order. Female sexuality is
thus often perceived as being dangerous, something to be
frightened of. Nevertheless, young women will usually be en-

couraged to form heterosexual relationships. Those who have difficulties in developing relationships with the opposite sex and women who realize they are homosexual may at this stage feel 'abnormal', lonely and depressed. These feelings may be exacerbated by the reactions of others:

When I was fourteen my school found out I was a lesbian and they weren't very happy about that. The deputy head rang my mother and asked her to come to the school immediately. ... That evening there was lots of tears and I got all the stuff that gay people get from their parents like 'where did we go wrong? Didn't we love you enough?' etc. etc. It was a very confusing time anyway — after years of being told certain things about relationships, it was all quite a shock and just trying to make sense of it all was quite difficult ... I had to go to see the deputy head and she wanted me to see the school doctor. I talked to the school doctor but she wanted me to see another doctor. My parents and I went along to this Child Guidance Clinic and I had to go into this room with a sign on the door saying 'Consultant Psychiatrist' and I really freaked, my first thought was 'my God, they think I'm mad!' — One of the first things she said was 'have I had a bang on the head?' ... and then I had to tell her about my 'problem' ... I was so confused because everyone else was treating it like a problem but the only problem I could see was that this girl didn't love me and no-one else understood my feelings for her. I started seeing this psychiatrist weekly and I was also sent to my G.P. for anti-depressants — by this time I was depressed.

Issues around identity development may be particularly difficult for young women. They are often caught between contradictory societal and familial expectations, for example of being a traditional woman and getting married as soon as possible, and of succeeding academically.

Conflicts of interest and of identity may be especially problematic for young women from ethnic minorities. Often they feel torn between two cultures, two sets of values and expectations, but feel alienated from both (Shaw 1983). West Indian girls have been found to experience particularly high and acute levels of identity confusion. They have difficulties in identifying both with their parents and with their own ethnic peer group. Their identity difficulties relate partly to their perceived lack of adequate female role-models (largely because of the 'invisibility' or negative stereotypes of black women in this society) and partly to the attitudes of their black male peers towards them (Numa 1984). Confusion over racial identity and self-image, as well as cultural conflicts, are also commonly experienced by young Asian women. Many people are now familiar with the way in which discord and dissension can sometimes develop in Asian families where the young woman may wish to be independent and sexually active (like her white English peers appear to be), but where her parents expect conformity to their own cultural and religious norms of female behaviour. An arranged marriage, or the prospect of one, occasionally leads such women to attempt suicide (CRE 1976; Malik 1983). This theme of adolescent conflict in Asian families is explored with great insight in the novel *Sumitra's Story* by Rukshana Smith (1982) and interestingly discussed in terms of social work intervention by Ahmed (1978, 1983).

The intense personal dilemmas of adolescence are affected by social and political issues. Factors such as racial discrimination, the availability of money, work, education, contraception, abortion and so on, affect the choices that can be made. With the present government clamping down on benefits for young people, reducing opportunities in further education and remaining complacent about unemployment, the choices for young people, especially women, seem to be narrowing. Facing a life on the dole, having to remain at home because of economic circumstances, and anticipating a nuclear holocaust are just a few of the factors that are causing some young people to despair. And the adolescents social workers see in the course of their work often have more reason to despair than most (see Crompton 1982).

Mid-life

The middle years are often times of change. Like all transitional stages they may herald the start of a new and creative life, but first there may be a period of intense mourning for what has been lost and a fearful anticipation of what is to come. The loss of children from the home at this time is often a significant event. For some women this brings much awaited freedom from the serving role, but for others, particularly those who were exclusively family-centred, the loss of children can leave a terrible vacuum in their lives with attendant feelings of point-lessness and worthlessness. Bart's study (1971) on depression in middle-aged women found that those who had wholeheartedly embraced the traditional roles of mother and wife and who had developed very close relationships with their children were par-ticularly prone to depression when their children left home. Jewish women were found to be especially likely to fall into this category. Having their raison d'être removed, these women suffered multiple losses: the loss of role, of self-esteem, of pur-pose and of meaningful relationships and experiences.

Middle-age may bring other changes and stresses for women. As Hemmings (1985) says:

> just as things start to ease with the children growing up, it's care of parents, the redundant or ailing husband, the bored and upset unemployed teenagers. All this just when we thought we might take a little time for ourselves, or simply get a job. (p. 6).

With the current Conservative government's policies of limiting public expenditure, encouraging familial responsibility and community care, increasing numbers of women are faced with *having* to care for relatives full time. And this, with little assistance from the state in the way of financial benefits or practical or emotional support (Jones and Vetter 1984). The role of full-time carer is not an easy one and women are likely to suffer exhaustion, a decrease in independence and privacy and, often, depression.

Middle-age may also bring a fear of old age. Patsy Murphy (1985) speaks for many when she says:

> I'm frightened of ... being on my own, having no-one to love, no-one loving me, not being able to manage, the fear that the whole structure that one calls one's life, which I often feel I have small control over, will collapse around me and that I won't have the health or the energy to put it together again ... My fear of old age is the fear of death ... I still cannot face the idea of my own death. (p.17).

For women, middle-age also means the menopause. While there is generally no *increased* risk of depression at this time, many women do feel vulnerable and low about the changes it implies. For those women who wanted children but were never able to have them, the final realization of the impossibility of conceiving may cause a deep depression. The cessation of periods may for some women also imply a loss of femininity, and with this sometimes comes fears of being no longer attractive, youthful and desirable. In a society that so over-values female attractiveness, growing older and losing youthful looks can be very depressing. As Norma Pitfield (1985) says 'older women are very conditioned to feeling self-disgust and the physical symptoms of the menopause can be construed to reinforce this' (p.170). Having headaches, hot flushes and pal-pitations may build up tension and contribute to, or exacerbate, feelings of depression and anxiety. While many women barely experience these symptoms, others may be overwhelmed by them. These women often feel that the depression they may experience accompanying such bodily changes is induced largely by the state of their hormones. One woman describes her experiences of oestrogen loss and the sudden onset of a baffling array of physical and psychological symptoms:

The beginning of the menopause for me was an awareness of aches and pains in every part of my body over a period of a few months, which I'd never had before and which depressed me. I thought I probably had cancer or something. I kept on having checks at my G.P. and I went to different doctors at different hospitals and the tests were always negative.... Finally I was referred to a specialist in HRT [hormone re-placement therapy] and the menopause and he explained that a lot of women begin to take a dive in their loss of oestrogen at any age from their late 30's, early 40's to late 50's – the age range is wide. Some people can lose oestrogen at an enormous rate and if they do their bones will be much more brittle when they're older, – but they know that HRT can arrest that physical effect. They can now measure oestrogen loss by taking a swab from the vagina. They did that test on me and I had a heavy oestrogen loss, so they said I definitely ought to have HRT. I started taking HRT, rather like the Pill, and that was the most extraordinary experience that I can remember from the menopause – within three days many of my symptoms [hair loss, eyesight deterioration, pains, depression] disappeared. It was incredibly dramatic. ... I continued taking it and realized I felt much better about myself – I felt my old self-confidence coming back again. I'm sure the loss of self-worth is to do with the chemical changes of the body because when I used to come off HRT for a while, I used to get those symptoms back again ... I used to feel so frightened that I couldn't do the things that before I would have done easily. I felt I'd be obliterated, that some terrible thing would happen to me, I don't know, it sounds absurd ... The anguish that I felt was that I'd lost myself, I wasn't me any longer, I used to feel desperate about it. I don't know if that's depression but it was certainly a sense of alienation because I just was not me any more ... I've felt much better since I'm over the menopause.

In most cases hormones will probably not be the sole cause of depression and so HRT may not be an effective means of dealing with this problem. An interaction between internal and external events is nearly always apparent, and other changes and factors associated with this stage of life may be equally significant. Some women writing in *Spare Rib* (Robertson 1983) explain the problem:

In common with many women, my menopause coincided with the death of my mother and the emergent adolescence/adulthood of the children I have parented. Both partings were painful and the loss of my mother a particularly protracted agony. The emotional and mental confusion at these events was hard to disentangle from the effects of my body's journey from pre- to post-menopause. (p.54).

...the worst symptom has been severe depression ... But I wasn't sure if it was the menopause or the fact that my close friend had died suddenly in Canada. I went to my own very sympathetic G.P. and told him my symptoms and about my friend's death, omitting that we'd been lovers. He found nothing wrong after a thorough check-up, but prescribed HRT, explaining that since I hadn't got a uterus there was no danger of womb cancer. So I took the pills for a month, and the minor symptoms, but not the depression, stopped. (p.55).

It would certainly seem worth investigating whether oestrogen loss is a significant factor in contributing to a woman's physical and psychological symptoms. At present, women at this life-stage are particularly subject to the often idiosyncratic opinions of GPs (Roberts 1985) who frequently react in one of three ways: They may pass off any difficulties by saying 'it's just the time of life' or 'it's women's problems' without offering any support or investigating further; they may say 'it's all psychological' and fail to do any physical examinations; or, they may say 'it's your hormones' and recommend a course of HRT without doing an oestrogen test or warning about the risks of cancer, or without looking into other explanations associated with life changes and social factors. None of these scenarios are satisfactory for the women concerned and they may cause them unnecessary misery. Women's problems at this life-stage, as at any other, need to be taken seriously.

The later years

Being old is not a problem in itself, although old age may be problematic for some. What are a problem, particularly for women, are the ageist attitudes held in this society. Ageism interacts negatively with sexism to produce a very oppressive force. Elderly men may be seen as wise and attractive but elderly women are typically viewed as 'old hags', 'old bags', 'old maids', and so on. The term 'an old woman' is used generally as an insult. If elderly women are not negatively stereotyped, they may be rendered totally invisible. Old people are rarely portrayed as people at all — they may be 'pensioners' or 'grannies' but rarely people with something valuable to contribute, and with opinions worth listening to. Further, they are regarded as sexless and hence not referred to (the social work literature included) in gender-related terms, they are simply 'the old'. This is despite the fact that the vast majority of over 65's are women. As Barbara Macdonald (Macdonald and Rich 1984) says:

> nothing told me that old women existed, or that it was possible to be glad to be an old woman. Again the silence held powerful and repressive messages (p.5).

This oppressive process of nullification may become internalized. It may erode an elderly woman's sense of self, lower her self-esteem and invalidate her as a person.

It may seem like a cliché to talk of the elderly in terms of being poor or lonely, but for elderly women this is often the reality. Elderly women, especially those who are unmarried, are more likely to be living in poverty than their male counterparts, owing to their restricted access to benefits and occupational pensions. They are also more likely to be living alone (Finch and Groves 1985) and while living alone does not *necessarily* mean being lonely and isolated, it quite often does. Further, elderly women living on their own are quite often in inadequate and substandard housing. Murphy (1982) has found that elderly women who are depressed are much more likely than other elderly women to be living on a meagre subsistence income and to have major housing problems. The relationship between these factors (that is, between environmental problems and depression) is probably causal. However, like Brown and Harris (1978), Murphy notes the importance of a confiding relationship as a mediating variable. Experiencing social problems, adverse life events and poor health are most likely to lead to depression if the elderly person also lacks an intimate relationship.

Loneliness and poverty may particularly affect elderly women from ethnic minorities, who, contrary to widely held expectations, do not always live with their families. They face the triple impact of sexism, ageism and racism. Services for elderly people, from residential homes to lunch clubs, to meals-on-wheels, are geared to the white majority — in terms of language, culture, diet, and so on — so that those from ethnic groups cannot comfortably make use of them. Indeed, many black elderly people live in fear of going into a home where they risk being the only non-white resident, misunderstood by the staff, perhaps unable to communicate with other residents, and forced to eat food they are unaccustomed to. Yet ethnic groups are rarely given the opportunity to set up and manage their own services. Furthermore, this group of elderly people are even more likely than others not to claim the benefits they are entitled to. This may be because of unfamiliarity with the system, language barriers, the fear of being seen as a 'burden on the state' or because of the stigma their own culture may attach to 'receiving charity'. Poverty in these cases is almost inevitable. Moreover, many black elderly people are not even registered with a GP. Thus they may not be receiving, or be able to make good use of, the most basic of services. Added to this is the isolation of just being black in a white society and the disillusion of growing old in a country from which they may feel alienated.

As one elderly West Indian is quoted as saying:

> There's no role for the elderly here. In the West Indies they're respected, they're involved in bringing up the children, and because they're older, they're thought of as wiser — people go to them for advice. But in this country, there's no respect. You're just an old person and nobody wants to know (Joseph 1985).

There are other aspects of being old which may make women vulnerable to depression. Loss is a recurrent issue in the lives of elderly people. Loss through the death of close ones is particularly likely and leads naturally to feelings of loneliness and depression. Parkes (1972) study on bereavement found that widows were more prone than widowers to emotional disturbance, because, he suggests, women's lives are more exclusively family-centred and therefore they are more devastated by the loss of a husband than are men by the loss of a wife.

Elderly people also experience a gradual loss of physical and mental agility. It can be very depressing to realise that one's memory and concentration are deteriorating, that one is becoming confused and disoriented, and no less painful emotionally to suffer aches and pains and the horrors of physical illness or disability. A lack of mobility plus failing eyesight and hearing can also add to the feeling of being cut off and isolated. For elderly women particularly, physical frailty means being even more vulnerable to violence and abuse from those within the family, or from men in the 'outside world'. As Cynthia Rich (1984) says: 'to be increasingly viewed with contempt by men proves no safeguard against rape. To be less physically strong and agile — or even to be perceived as such — makes us ready targets for male violence'. (p.60).

For those elderly people who go to live in residential care, and women are more likely to do so than men (Finch and Groves 1985), loss is again a central theme. Their own home, security and familiarity, their privacy, dignity and independence are generally all mourned for. Each successive loss that an elderly person experiences brings her closer to the ultimate loss of life itself. Anxiety about one's own death is often only a further stress in the lives of elderly people, which together with all the other stresses make them so particularly vulnerable to depression.

There certainly seem to be many reasons why elderly people might get depressed, yet depression in this age group is frequently overlooked. Depressive symptoms may simply be regarded as characteristic of old age or confused with various organic states. Nevertheless, depression is still apparently the most common 'psychiatric disorder' found in the elderly and is as distressing at this time as it is in younger people (Epstein 1976). Once it is recognized for what it is, there is no reason to be any less optimistic about the possibilities for overcoming depression in this age group than in any other.

Life-situations and life-crises

We shall now look at a variety of situations in which women may become vulnerable to depression. Although we have highlighted the depressing aspects of various circumstances and experiences, this is not intended to imply that depression is in any way a necessary or inevitable part of them.

Marriage, housework and child-care

Research has shown that although married people of both sexes are less likely to experience mental illness and depression than unmarried people, marriage is significantly more of a protector for men than for women (Gove 1972; Gove and Tudor 1973; Pearlin and Johnson 1977). This abrogates the myth that marriage is equally fulfilling for both partners. But what is it that makes the experience less satisfying for women? Both men and women tend to have unrealistically high expectations of marriage, often believing that it will fulfill every need — for love, friendship, support, sexual satisfaction and so on. However, men's needs are more likely to be met, since they are generally better at asking for what they want and since women are more sensitive to and accustomed to meeting the needs of others than men are. Also, men are in fact much less likely to have to depend solely on women for the satisfaction of their needs, since they tend to retain relationships and opportunities outside of marriage, through the world of work. In contrast, married women, especially those with young children, are often totally dependent on men emotionally as well as financially. A woman may even find that her own personal identity is completely submerged in her relationships with her husband and children. Such a vulnerable position may lead to feelings of frustration, lack of fulfillment, and low self-esteem. Since women have not usually learned assertive ways of communicating and dealing with conflicts they frequently swallow, or deny, their feelings of resentment and frustration. For women have been taught that for them to show anger and rage is unfeminine and hence undesirable. Anger thus becomes a much feared emotion, and is turned inward, rather than outward. Depression is often the consequence.

Other reasons for women's relatively poor mental health in marriage are related to their social role. In particular, the role of housewife is considered to be inherently stressful (Gove and Tudor 1973; Oakley 1974, 1976). In addition to restricting women to finding their major source of satisfaction within the family, the job of housewife tends to be routine, monotonous and frustrating, and being relatively unstructured allows time for brooding over troubles. Furthermore, housework affords little social prestige, is rarely acknowledged or appreciated and seems like a never-ending job when whatever is done can immediately be undone. It is taken for granted as 'women's work' and rewarded neither by pay nor recognition.

> I went down as usual after C was in bed to clear up. But then I thought there's no point in clearing up because she's only going to make the same mess tomorrow as she did today, and then the next day and the day after, it seemed endless. I sat on the chair, I thought there's no point in going to bed 'cause I'll only have to make it again tomorrow so I just sat there, for maybe three days, I don't know how long — till the social worker broke in with the police...

The additional tasks of caring for children, which are undoubtedly gratifying and fulfilling in some respects, may also contribute to a woman's burden. Feelings of continual exhaustion and frustration are not uncommon for women who look after children all day. A recent, though small scale study (Piachaud 1984) found that on average child-care tasks took over seven hours a day, that 89 per cent of this time was spent by women and that 64 per cent of mothers said they did not even have one hour a week free from the responsibility of the children.

Feelings of exhaustion and frustration are often compounded by loneliness and isolation. Many mothers find themselves in housing estates with few amenities and little community life and at a great distance from their family or friends. With only their children for company they may feel driven to despair:

> After having my second baby I got really depressed. I was tired anyway but the depression made it worse, my body felt so heavy and it wouldn't work properly, it was as if I was paralysed. I had no-one to help me and no-one to talk to, and I think I was driven mad by loneliness. The doctor told me to go out and meet people and to take plenty of rest. But with two children it's not easy. I still have to wash their nappies, do the housework, feed them, change them, play with them. I can't have lots of rest!

> The loneliest time is when the kids have gone to bed and you're sitting on your own in a high-rise flat and you don't know nobody and you've got no-one to talk to. There's a hell of a lot of women out there like that, but at the time I didn't realize it, I thought I was the only one.

Caring for children is seen as women's 'natural function' and hence they are expected to take on full responsibility for the job. Men rarely see child-care as part of their role and little provision is made by the state for young children. Thus women feel guilty if they believe they are not coping adequately, or not enjoying child-care. Images from the media of smiling mothers, spotless children and well-fed husbands reinforce such feelings of guilt and inadequacy and encourage the belief that women's experiences of frustration and despair are manifestations of their own personal failings.

The vulnerable position of women looking after children has been corroborated by research. Moss and Plewis (1977) found that 52 per cent of their sample of mothers with pre-school children had a moderate or severe 'distress problem'. Richman (1977) found that 39 per cent of mothers of three year olds with a 'behaviour problem' and 26 per cent of mothers of children without such problems, were depressed. In another study (Richman 1974) 41 per cent of mothers living in council housing with at least two children of three and under were severely or moderately depressed. Those who lived in flats (high or low rise) were more prone to loneliness, isolation and depression than those in houses.

Marriage and, particularly, motherhood generally entails

economic dependency on men or the state. Many assume that because women make up 40 per cent of the workforce this is not the case. However, the facts are that 42 per cent of married women do not work outside the home and this number increases to 51 per cent of married women with children (Chester 1985). Mothers employed outside the home tend to be those whose children are at least of school age. Approximately 70 per cent of women with children under five do not work outside the home at all (Martin and Roberts 1984). Further, mothers who are in employment tend to be working part-time. Since wages earned on part-time work are rarely sufficient to support anyone, women still remain dependent on men or the state to make up their income. What all this amounts to is that despite assumptions about changes in family patterns and women's roles over the years, most women are still essentially in a dependent position and undoubtedly take the major, if not the sole, responsibility for housework and child-care. Dependency is often coupled with poverty (Townsend 1979). Both poverty and dependence are likely to increase the risk of depression (Belle 1982, Brown and Harris 1978). These factors, especially when combined with oppressive attitudes and practices towards women, can make marriage and/or family life little more than a trap for many women:

> We had a difficult relationship from the start but I thought it was all my fault, that I wasn't being a good wife and that if I tried harder and cleaned the flat better and cooked better meals and so on, then everything would get better. Eventually, I began to realize that it was a sort of crisis of rising expectations so that the better I got at whatever it was, the criticisms switched to other areas, but I was lumbered ... I wanted to leave but there was this awful thing that I couldn't find out how much money I could get, I couldn't get any idea whatsoever, and there was no way I could be self-supporting on my income alone. I just felt completely trapped by financial considerations and the fact that I had two small children meant that I had to have a certain amount of money to be able to manage with them.

> We'd only been married a few months when he started drinking heavily and abused me physically and mentally ... before we were married we were living together in A— and it

was fine, really happy, it was a bed of roses. But then (he told me later) he thought he had me over a barrel, he thought he could do what he wanted with me and get away with it because I had no money, no friends there, and no-one to turn to for help, so I was completely stuck ...

I suffered mental cruelty for about fifteen years ... it got so as I used to believe all the awful things he was telling me and that made me depressed ... Just him coming home at night made me feel depressed ... whatever time of night he came home — usually drunk — I had to make him dinner — he just expected it because I was his wife, I was bought and paid for and had to provide the goods whether I wanted to or not — cook his dinner, keep his clothes and keep his bed regardless of my feelings ... I phoned the Samaritans once but they couldn't help and there wasn't anyone else to help 'cause when you're low and down no-one wants to know you. I did leave three times but I went back because I was scared — fear makes you go back. The thought of never getting a house, or bringing the four kids up on my own scared me, though I'd been doing that anyway. But actually standing alone makes you more afraid.

It would be wrong to imply that marriage and family life is necessarily bleak and unrewarding for women. Indeed, a relationship built on equality and intimacy and that offers love, support and companionship can provide an excellent shield against depression.

Motherhood

The birth of a child can be a joyous and wonderful occasion. Nevertheless, it is frequently associated with depression in mothers. Estimates suggest that 'clinical post-natal depression' affects 15–24 per cent of new mothers (Oakley 1980). Medical practice tends to assume that hormones play the greatest part in the causation of this problem, yet research proving this has not been conclusive (Oakley 1980). In addition to any endocrinological explanations, sociological factors must be considered. Depression after childbirth seems likely to be associated with difficulties in negotiating the transition to motherhood, plus the stressful nature of women's lives at this time. Most new mothers, much to their chagrin, do not conform to stereotypical images of living in maternal bliss. Instead, they are usually struggling to adjust to a taxing new life-style, where sleepless nights, and crying, demanding babies are the rule, not the exception. The vulnerability of new babies is likely to invoke anxiety, their constant demands can lead to feelings of fragmentation and submerged identity, and their incessant crying can engender a sense of inadequacy. The strong emotions that babies evoke in mothers, coupled with the immense practical demands, can often leave a mother feeling exhausted, hopeless and unable to cope. Vivienne Welburn's book on postnatal depression (1980) gives an excellent account of these problems and those arising from trying to juggle with the conflicting demands of baby, husband and housework. It tells too, how such difficulties can lead to and be exacerbated by isolation. For the efforts involved in going out and socialising — preparing the baby, fitting in feeds, struggling with public transport — may not seem worth making. Isolation often leads to loneliness. Together these factors can easily lead to depression:

> My baby was unplanned. When I had him I didn't know what to do and there was no-one around to help me. My husband was around sometimes but he doesn't know much about babies and all my family are back in Africa. So I had to do everything myself and it was hard. Before I could go out I had to get the pram and two kids down all the stairs. It was too much so I usually didn't bother. I stayed home and talked to the walls getting more and more lonely and depressed.

For many women, particularly those who have been working, the arrival of a new baby may be accompanied by a sense of loss — loss of independence, relative freedom, social contacts, status, earnings and perhaps an exclusive relationship with a partner. Such losses may or may not be compensated for by the birth of the baby.

Research has also found that depression after childbirth is associated with facets of the actual birth experience. A medium to high level of technology, a low degree of maternal control and dissatisfaction with birth management have been found to result in depression in many cases (Oakley 1980).

> I had a very difficult birth ... I was in labour for such a long time that I went into shock. I kept asking the midwife for an

epidural but she kept refusing saying I'd be all right. Finally they called the doctor and he gave me one. A student came too and they were doing internals — I thought it was going to be a woman but it was a man, and I was so embarrassed but I couldn't say anything and I was stuck with my legs in stirrups and I didn't have anyone with me ... When G. was born they didn't tell me anything was wrong and they took him straight off to the nursery. I had him for about two minutes, and 'cause of the epidural my arms had gone dead and I couldn't hold him, but they said they didn't have time to hold my arms so I could hold him, so they took him off and I didn't realize how bad he was. That evening he was put into Special Care, I couldn't feed him, he had to have a drip. I didn't see him for two days because he was put into B block and I was in A block and they didn't have a bed there ... I was really scared and thought I'd lose him as I'd lost one already, I was convinced he was going to die ... I think all that contributed to my post-natal depression.

For women who are unable to conceive, post-natal depression may seem like a small price to pay for a baby. Women who are childless, for whatever reason, may feel that they are missing out on an apparently essential aspect of womanhood. Because women are socialized to be maternal and to produce children, motherhood is always an issue they have to face. A social stigma still attaches to childless women regardless of whether childlessness is a choice or not. This stigma plus the disappointment and sense of loss that women who are forced to be childless often experience, can engender feelings of guilt, inadequacy and depression. Similarly, women whose children are involuntarily removed from their care can feel hopeless, impotent, useless and desperate. Their function and role in life which, it is assumed, all women should fulfil, and fulfil expertly, is stripped from them. They become, in their own and society's eyes, worthless and valueless.

Motherhood is a difficult issue for lesbian women too. Whether to have children or not may be a hard choice to make, as it is for many women, but how to conceive if they do want them is obviously especially problematic. Once they become mothers, lesbian women often face fear, isolation and hostility since they are operating outside the values of heterosexual society. Challenging the traditional norms of family life may mean that they live in fear of losing custody of their children and/or losing their children's respect:

> When P sees us being affectionate she seems to give us a look of disdain. She's got to the age when she wants to be in a 'normal family' and is embarrassed by the fact that she isn't.

> We live in a small place in the country and most of the time we're pretty scared, like will people mistreat the children?... when their friends suddenly can't make it for tea I wonder whether an adult has stepped in ... Then we worry about custody. What would happen if D came back and tried to get the children? Lesbian mothers lose custody really easily.

Single women

Single people are more at risk of depression than married people, although single women seem to be slightly less vulnerable than single men (Gove 1972, Pearlin and Johnson 1977). Their psychological distress may in part be related to a lack of an intimate and confiding relationship (Brown and Harris 1978). Yet being single does not necessarily exclude women from such relationships and having a partner does not necessarily imply a high degree of support and intimacy. Nevertheless, single women may feel a sense of apparent 'deviancy' in a society that prizes marriage so highly. Such deviancy has particular significance for women since they are generally only considered to be successful as women once they have 'connected' themselves to a man (Eichenbaum and Orbach 1982). Through this connection, especially when it is sealed by marriage, women usually derive their social status, title, name and perhaps, even, their sense of identity and purpose. Without this relationship, women can feel incomplete, 'odd' and vulnerable, especially when they have not chosen their single status. The achievement of psychological autonomy is frequently problematic for women. These psychological difficulties tend to be exacerbated and reinforced by social ones. Being single can be a stigma in a couple-oriented society and women may feel out of place and excluded from many activities. Although it is now more acceptable for women to remain on their own, images of single women are still sometimes negative. Even those who remain single through choice, may be assumed to be unmarried because of their personal failure to 'catch' a man. Hence they are often viewed as objects of pity or scorn and labelled as 'old maids' and 'on the shelf'.

Adapting to being single after being in a relationship may be particularly stressful. Indeed, research indicates that formerly married people have higher rates of depression than those who have never been married (Pearlin and Johnson 1977). This may be associated with difficulties in coping with new demands, adjusting to new role definitions, abandoning familiar life-styles and relationships and suffering a blow to self-image and esteem. Whether people were married or not, however, the experience of a relationship break-up is likely to lead to feelings of abandonment, loss, emptiness and loneliness. The absence of a partner may leave a vacuum of unmet psychological, social and sexual needs. According to Maggie Scarf (1981), women are especially prone to respond with depression to a loss or threatened loss of a love-bond because they have invested so much more of themselves, of their own 'inner substance' in them.

I felt completely lost when P left. We had done everything together and I had got out of the habit of seeing my other friends regularly. I was also totally dependent on him emotionally and found I had no-one to confide in after he had gone. So it was like my whole world fell apart when he left . . .

In addition to these psychological demands and pressures, single women experience ongoing strains and stresses that are related to socio-structural conditions. Problems of poverty and isolation are augmented for single women, who are more likely to respond to such conditions with depression than their married sisters (Pearlin and Johnson 1977). For single mothers these stresses are added to by burdensome child-care responsibilities. Two women explain some of the difficulties of being a single parent:

When I first had the children I never used to see anyone for weeks on end. I was on my own but not on my own as there was never any time away from the kids, so I couldn't be what I wanted to be ... I didn't seem to even have time for a shower, or even one hour on my own when I could do what I wanted.

I'd love to go out more but I don't have the money to pay for
a baby-sitter ... I cash my giro on a Monday and straight
away I pay the gas, electric, mortgage overdraft and buy the
food, and I'm left with 23 pence. I don't have any money to
enjoy myself unless I take some from the bill money, and then
I have to go without a few meals and buy less food so I can
put it back. If it wasn't for my mum always buying the boys'
shoes ...

A recent study (Letts 1983) found that single-parent mothers
are in a particularly disadvantageous position because they bear
a double handicap: they are vulnerable to the social and sexual
discrimination against all women as well as to the discrimination against those who do not fit into the conventional pattern
of the nuclear family. They are discriminated against in areas of
finance, employment, housing and health care.

Work and unemployment

Research has shown that paid work can protect women against
depression since it can provide a source of income and social
contacts, alleviate boredom, and raise self-esteem. (Weissman
and Paykel 1974, Brown and Harris 1978). Yet, this does not
mean that paid work is always rewarding. Many jobs done by
women are just as lacking in status and tedious as those done in
the home. Typically, women are underpaid, undervalued and
provided with little opportunity for influencing the work process. They often find themselves in jobs that are not commensurate with their educational backgrounds and they may
have to work harder than men to achieve the same level of
promotion, recognition or status. Furthermore, women often
feel fraught with conflicts in their working role; they may fear
success, feel guilty about leaving their children, or even about
taking a 'man's job'. They may also be subject to sexual harrass-
ment or other pressures at work. Thus while employment may
sometimes be beneficial and rewarding to women, it may also
contribute to stress and serve to reinforce feelings of impotence
and low self-worth.

Paid employment outside the home is of course usually particularly complicated for mothers. Full-time jobs do not fit in
with the demands and needs of children and so provision has to
be made for them either for all or part of the day. The general
lack of state facilities means that such provision usually has to

be paid for, often out of meagre resources. Ensuring adequate child-care tends to be a continuing source of anxiety to working mothers and the additional tasks of attending to children before and after a full working day can be demanding and exhausting. Many women compromise of course, by getting part-time work, although it is obviously financially less rewarding, less secure and offers fewer perks and opportunities for career development than full-time work. Furthermore, it does not totally eradicate the problems of child-care.

The type and amount of work in combination with the personality of an individual woman and the availability of child-care facilities are all crucial considerations in determining whether employment will increase or decrease vulnerability to depression. Here are some women's views about the value or otherwise of paid employment:

My doctor persuaded me that I'd feel better if I got out the house and took a job. I gave in and got a part-time job. But it didn't solve the problem. It was boring and tiring and with all the child-care arrangements I just felt it wasn't worth it. It didn't make me feel any better, so I packed it in.

I'd decided it was the best thing for me to continue to work because I was afraid that if I'd stayed in the new town we'd just moved to with a new baby I would get really depressed and also I thought I'd never be able to get back to work because I'd lose confidence. I think I got less depressed than I would have done if I'd stayed at home, but I felt awful leaving this tiny baby in her crib with the child-minder and I always felt she wasn't being looked after quite as well as I would have looked after her. I felt just terribly guilty, but managed to suppress it.

My job is making me feel very stressed and it's very exhausting. I can feel myself getting lower and lower and sinking into a depression, though work keeps me going and prevents me from collapsing and cracking up altogether.

Once I started working my depression began to lift and I felt a lot better.

Losing a job, or being unemployed when one wants to work,

can be a very depressing experience, especially apparently, for single women (Warr and Parry 1982). The concept of unemployment is usually related to men but women can feel equally inadequate about not getting work, and equally hopeless about years on the dole. The erosion of self-confidence that can derive from being without a job, the sense of futility and worthlessness, the boredom and often the loneliness, can be very intense. Living on the breadline does not help matters either. It severely limits the opportunities available and puts an added strain upon every aspect of life. Poverty usually means living at the margins of society for one cannot afford to engage in so many of the activities that people with money take for granted. These women express some of the feelings common to many unemployed people:

One of the most shocking things about unemployment was that it very quickly took away a lot of my confidence — in a matter of a month or so. And because I wasn't well I couldn't go out and do things, so I got quite isolated — it's very socially isolating to be unemployed and disabled. So when it comes to thinking about getting jobs and working with people it's actually quite frightening to think that I've got to go out there and be with people again.

A really depressing thing about being unemployed is coping with the unpredictable mood swings. One time I can feel quite content, feel it's all OK, but in the next few hours it can change and I think 'God! What am I doing with my life?' I've spent six years training to do something and now I'm not doing it.

One of the most difficult things about unemployment is looking towards the future, because you think there'll be endless weeks of doing the same thing, of doing almost nothing. Although I kept myself busy doing things, there was never anything concrete to show for it at the end of the day. I think our society puts so much emphasis on purposeness — your life's got to have an aim and purpose, and you've got to be going out and doing things for other people, that it's awful if you don't. You're made to feel that spending all day on yourself is wrong, is selfish, but it's what you have to do when you're unemployed.

Sometimes I've been in a real panic about being unemployed. I feel as if my brain cells are rapidly dying and sometimes I feel as if I've got absolutely nothing to talk about, nothing to offer — It's losing confidence in yourself which is a really horrible feeling.

Traumatic life events and violence towards women

Research indicates that psychological distress such as depression is closely correlated with the number and intensity of stressful life events that a person experiences (Paykel *et al* 1969; Freden 1982). Interestingly, however, stressful events such as rape, sexual assault or abortion, which only women experience, have not generally been included in studies. We assume, nevertheless, that these violent experiences, and those such as abortion, miscarriage, mastectomy and hysterectomy are very stressful, traumatic and painful and are likely to be linked to depression. A woman generally has to mourn the loss of her baby, womb or breast, work through the implications of the loss for her life and sense of self, and adapt to the changes that it brings. Depression may be an inevitable part of the mourning and healing process. However, sometimes the depressed reaction may be prolonged and severe.

I miscarried at 28 weeks — the baby was perfectly formed. The medical reasons for why I miscarried weren't clear — the doctors said different things so it was very confusing. I didn't know what to think and I got really depressed ... I had a lot of guilt about it because I thought that I'd actually pre-cipitated the miscarriage by my feelings of emotional anger towards my boyfriend. I kept balancing between total depression and anger ... It's left me with very strong feelings that I want another child but now I'm not in a relationship and I don't want to be a single parent. I've had to resign myself to never having children as I'm now 37. I'm actually quite fatalistic about it now.

Having an abortion was a really traumatic experience which I think I never really got over, partly because I wasn't able to talk about it at the time. None of the doctors or nurses spoke to me about it - either before or afterwards, it was like a closed book, a taboo subject. They didn't even ask if I wanted the baby at all. It was so awful because you have to keep all your thoughts and feelings to yourself. I couldn't see the baby either and I really wanted to. I wanted to be able to say goodbye to it.

An experience of violence such as rape can have profound repercussions for a woman's life-style, her self-perception, feelings of self-worth and sense of mastery. Typical reactions to all forms of male violence include feelings of self-doubt and self-blame, guilt, worthlessness, impotence and fear, as well as depression:

After my husband had nearly killed me and the children and I'd got away, I got really depressed. I got lower and lower and hit rock bottom. I wasn't sleeping or eating or what I was eating just came back up because I couldn't digest my food. I lay in the hospital bed, petrified of every man that walked in, wondering what I was going to do. The depression was so deep I couldn't see any hope at all, I just gave up, I lay there and thought I wanted to die.

He always expected me to have sex with him whether I wanted it or not. It got to the stage where if I did say no he'd take me anyway ... he'd just pin me down and that would be it, I'd just have to lay there and take it even if I cried 'cause he was hurting me ... there's no such thing as rape in marriage and I just had to put up with it, I was powerless.

People wonder why I didn't leave earlier, and why I let it go on and I ask myself that a lot too, I sometimes blame myself, but it's just such a big amount of fear 'cause you're so under the control of someone and you want to survive and your only way to survive is to just let them control you ... I really wanted to escape often, but I was always scared to in case I got punished for it, because the last time I tried to run away he burnt my feet and I couldn't walk for a month afterwards and that cut my freedom down even more ... Now I'm really scared to go out and I'm really frightened of men ... I just don't know who I am — all along I was told I belonged to my father and brother but since I left home I don't belong to anyone ... I've always had to be so many different people, that now I don't know who I am.

Frequently women's feelings of guilt and depression seem to be reinforced by the institutions supposedly poised to help female 'victims', such as the police, legal system and the health and personal social services. For often, these agencies treat women unsympathetically and accuse them of being responsible for the acts of cruelty towards them. Such attitudes contribute to women's oppression and probably depression. They condone, minimize or excuse male violence and perpetuate the likelihood of abuse:

> I told my GP what had happened, how he nearly killed us all and he just said 'well, you're no angel either' because he'd just been listening to my husband saying I wouldn't hug and kiss him. When the police came in I asked them to arrest my husband for attempted murder, but they said they couldn't do that because it was a domestic dispute.

> After I was raped and came back to the hospital some of the nurses said some really horrible things to me. One of them asked me to tell her 'all the gory details' and she treated it as if it was a big joke. There was only one nurse who came up to me afterwards and hugged me or paid me any attention 'cause I was really upset. My doctor kept asking me if I was lying and when I said that anyone could get raped, even her, she said 'no I couldn't because I wouldn't be so stupid.' Everyone made me feel it was all my fault. The police decided not to prosecute after they spoke to my consultant even though they had evidence of intercourse and knew the man had raped another woman.

In addition to any particular acts of cruelty towards them, women carry throughout their lives a sense of their vulnerability to male violence. At any stage they may be subject to sexual abuse, physical attack or rape, both from within the family and outside of it. The continual threat of, or susceptibility to violence is stressful in itself and deprives women of choices and full control over life-options. Women often feel, for instance, that they have to restrict where they go, especially at night, that they have to be careful about how they dress and about what they say or do in front of men. Fear can become an integral part of women's lives.

Disablement

The sudden onset of a serious illness or disablement pre-
cipitates a tremendous crisis to the individual — one which has
many and far-reaching implications:

> Firstly, I had to face the no-hope situation — that I'd be like
> this for life. I had to get used to being dependent and not
> having the control over life that I had. I had to give up my
> job, move house and change my life-style in loads of ways.
> My relationship with friends and the outside world changed.
> I just lost all my confidence in myself and got really
> depressed.

One woman talks of her depressing experiences of being ill,
experiences which must be common to many:

> The first month or so of being ill it wasn't so bad, but it's the
> long-term thing which is most depressing. I spent nearly six
> months being completely housebound. It was so, so strange
> just to be on my own for hours and hours in the same room.
> Sometimes I thought I was going to go mad and I used to hit
> the walls and things out of frustration. I got very bad
> claustrophobia and I wanted to push the walls back because
> they used to move in sometimes and I longed to go out and
> get into the country but was not able to. My social space
> shrunk, life centred in that room, so when I finally did get out
> it was a real shock — the brightness, the noise and the smell
> of the traffic made me feel as if I was going to faint, it was so
> big and vast. It made me want to run back in again to the
> comfort of that room ... At first friends used to come round
> but after a while they stopped coming because I wasn't
> getting any better, it was getting boring and I didn't have
> *anything* to talk about and that would really upset me because
> I became a boring person. The only thing I could talk about
> was my back and people would see me in terms of my back
> and that was strange. People wouldn't say how are *you*, they'd
> say how's your back, and I became M the back, rather than a
> person ... It was a great strain on our relationship ...
> Sometimes I'd get so depressed that I couldn't talk, I
> couldn't do anything and he'd ask what was wrong, but I
> couldn't actually articulate it, because when you feel like that
> you just can't and I just went right into myself. That was very

difficult for him to understand and he'd get angry with me and that would make me worse. Also, it was very difficult for me to be dependent on a man as I'd spent most of my life trying to be independent, and he didn't have any obligations towards me. And because he was a man people would say 'isn't he wonderful, he's marvellous, he does all the cooking, the cleaning and the shopping!' and they'd actually make me feel more guilty and yet if it had been reversed I'm sure they wouldn't have had the same wonderment ... After a year I'd resigned myself to being like this for the rest of my life, which was another depressing thing, because I lost my fight and stopped being angry and became very passive, letting it wash over me. It was the only way I could cope. I adapted to being disabled and I was taking on a disabled outlook — I was becoming quite happy to have things done for me. So it became quite difficult to start doing things on my own again...

People with disabilities also have to face discrimination and prejudice and the fear or curiosity that the able-bodied express towards them. To be or become disabled in this society seems to mean that one is devalued as a person, considered brainless, and sometimes rendered totally invisible (witness the 'does she take sugar' attitude). Physical impairment also means experiencing systematic segregation and isolation. Disabled people are denied access to most places and hence excluded from full participation in many aspects of life. Disability is thus in a sense bestowed upon people by society. As one woman says:

Disability can and sometimes does interfere with the practical running of a life but it is the reaction and non-action of a society which causes disablement. (Sue, in Campling 1981, p.48).

Like black people and women, another woman notes, the disabled are an 'oppressed group':

segregated and substandard education, a physical environment that does not take our needs into account, job discrimination, housing discrimination, lack of aids and services and the threat of institutionalisation keep us dependent and always ready to please. (Merry, in Campling 1981, p.30).

Merry notes too how she had 'taken in so many of these oppressive ideas and values' and that the 'oppression of women and the oppression of those who are disabled comes together'. For since society did not see her as a 'real' woman, she did not really see herself as one. Another woman explains further the possible problems that a woman with disabilities may face:

> She may feel that she is no longer sexually attractive or lovable; her self-confidence, which is strongly linked to her conception of the image she wishes to project of herself and which represents how she intends society to regard her, is seriously shaken. She feels ugly, faulty, impaired and worthless. (Barbara, in Campling 1981, p.44).

Women from ethnic minorities

Women from ethnic minorities experience problems common to all women but these are added to and intensified by the existence of racism. Women 'of colour' tend to be disproportionately located in the poorest sectors of the community. Here the stress of poverty is largely caused, aggravated and perpetuated by racial prejudice in such vital areas as housing, employment, education and health services. The consequences of such prejudice are, for example, that women from ethnic minorities have higher rates of unemployment than white women and when they are in work, are more likely to be in low-status, low-paid jobs or jobs that are not commensurate with their educational attainments (Edmonds 1982). Chronic disappointment and frustration are likely to be experienced when strivings for social advancement and improved life-circumstances are continually blocked by racial as well as sexual discrimination. Institutionalized racism is compounded by frequent and sometimes violent personal attacks on all people 'of colour'. Black and Asian women may live in fear for themselves, their children, family and friends.

The racism penetrating almost every aspect of British life and society (from the language used, to media images and police practices) is extremely hurtful to black and other ethnic minority peoples and can have the cumulative effect of destroying a person's self-respect and self-esteem. For prejudice is not always just experienced as an onslaught from outside, as simply an external constraint. Often it becomes part of an individual's self-image, an image defined by others (Littlewood and

Lipsedge 1982). Thus over time, blacks, Asians and others may, like many women, have internalized their oppression and developed a psychology suitable to an oppressed group. They may carry with them a profound sense of inferiority and worthlessness. This sense of inferiority is often expressed in terms of a deep desire to be and belong to the white, dominant culture, sometimes to the point of totally denying their own cultural identity in order to 'identify with the oppressor':

As a child I always had dreams of waking up as a white child and always had fantasies of being adopted really and being white, English really. I used to dream I'd wake up and peel off all the layers of skin to find I was white underneath. I think those dreams are quite common to coloured children.

My mother never wears saris any more, she always wears trousers. She's cut her hair short as well, it's as if she's trying to shrug off her identity. In fact she doesn't even look Indian because she's so pale, because she's never gone out in the sun, she wouldn't dream of it. She just wouldn't want to go any blacker.

Some of the Asian people at college are terribly English, they've thrown off all their identity; they look more English than a lot of English people do in their clothes and haircuts etc. They've just tried to ignore the fact they're Asian, which I think I've also done to a certain extent.

This identification with the dominant white culture may also be an attempt to be less conspicuous, with the aim of avoiding racial attack. The problem is, however, that anyone without a white skin is not allowed to forget the fact:

You can just be walking down the street or in a shop or pub or somewhere and you can be subject to abuse and every time you feel terribly hurt by it, it's a constant reminder...

Black, Asian and other ethnic minority women who are recent immigrants to these shores also face the stress of trying to adapt to a new and often inhospitable environment, where the language, customs, culture, climate and diet may all be unfamiliar. Those who have had to leave behind them their spouse, children and other family and friends are deprived of their usual support systems and thus may face additional feelings of loss and insecurity. They may experience many years of anxiety while waiting to be reunited with other family members. Immigrants also often live under the continual fear of deportation.

Asian women have been noted to be at particular risk of depression and emotional breakdown (CRE 1976). Those who do not work outside the home (more typically Muslim women) can become chronically lonely and isolated, especially if they speak little English or are not living among people from their own ethnic community. The lack of support available to these and other ethnic minority women, coupled with the shortage of interpreters or information in their own languages, can lead many to feel overwhelmed, worthless and alienated. Such feelings may be exacerbated if their children, who have learnt English in school, are unwilling to communicate with them in their mother tongue.

Asian women who do go out to work (more commonly Hindu and Sikh women) are faced, like other women, with the double burden of having two jobs. However, this situation may be more stressful for Asian women, since traditionally they are expected to entertain visitors and cook for large numbers at home, and usually face more adverse working conditions in their jobs. Conflicts often develop in Asian families where husbands fail to appreciate the stresses that their wives, working or not, are under.

While life in Britain may be difficult and depressing for immigrant Asian and other ethnic minority women, the prospect of returning to their country of origin may not be desirable, feasible or possible. If they do wish to leave Britain they may have to face the very real stigma of 'failure'. Women in these situations can easily end up feeling trapped and depressed. Many experience intense disappointment as they find their hopes and dreams for a better quality of life shattered.

There are innumerable reasons why ethnic minority women living in Britain may get depressed. Indeed, like their white sisters, evidence has shown that they are more prone to depression than their male counterparts (Littlewood and Lipsedge 1982). The few community surveys that there are also indicate that the incidence of depression, especially amongst Asian women, is quite high (CRE 1976; Ali Khan 1983).

Furthermore, a study by Burke (1984) found that West Indian women in inner city areas had higher rates of depression than their white British counterparts. Since the differential was statistically significant it 'suggests that racial pressure is a causatory factor in depression' (Burke 1984, p.60). Yet the significance of racism is frequently underplayed by professionals. Despite the evidence of high incidence rates of depression in ethnic minority peoples it often remains unrecognized and undiagnosed. This may in part be explained by the suggestion that depressed Asian and Afro-Caribbean people are more likely than white people to present with physical symptoms, and Africans are less likely to have suicidal or guilty thoughts (Littlewood and Lipsedge 1982). Thus depression may be masked and hence misdiagnosed because of the presence or absence of specific symptoms which are themselves culturally specific. The needs of ethnic minorities may again fail to be attended to by a racially unjust society.

Summary

We have explored in this chapter a few of the many complex factors that may lead women to be depressed. Some of these relate to women's experiences at particular life-stages, others to crisis situations, or to the overall quality of their lives and relationships. Women's susceptibility to depression seems to be related to their frequently low self-image, to their vulnerability to violence and the effects of loss, and to the often limited, constraining and unsatisfying roles they fulfil in society. Such roles typically remain unrecognized and unrewarded. Socialization experiences are also important for protecting or exposing women to depression. Stereotypical patterns of socialization do not seem to equip females adequately for dealing with stress in later life. In particular, the fact that women have for centuries been brought up to feel that they are second-class citizens, inferior to men, induces feelings of helplessness and low self-esteem, which are later reinforced by messages from the media and society generally. While this may be changing slowly, many women have already internalized these messages and have come to believe in them. Because of this, women's own inner feelings of helplessness can reinforce and perpetuate their relative powerlessness in the external world.

The focus in this chapter on the depressing aspects of women's experiences does not of course mean that women never gain any satisfaction or derive pleasure from their lives. But the very fact of being a woman in today's society entails coping with a variety of stresses and restrictions which can all too easily lead to depressive episodes. However, there are some factors that seem to be particularly helpful in protecting women from depression. These are positive early experiences; an androgynous identity; a confiding, intimate and equal relationship; a satisfying and rewarding paid job; and adequate support networks.

Further reading

Here are some general books which are on, or refer to women's mental health and/or to women and depression specifically:

Archer, J. and Lloyd, B. (1982) *Sex and Gender*, Harmondsworth: Penguin.

Belle, D. (ed.) (1982) *Lives in Stress*, New York: Sage.

Brown, G.W. and Harris, T. (1978) *Social Origins of Depression*, London: Tavistock Publications.

Fransella, F. and Frost, K. (1977) *Women: On Being a Woman*, London: Tavistock Publications.

Guttentag, M., Salasin, S. and Belle, D. (1980) *The Mental Health of Women*, New York: Academic Press.

Howell, E. and Bayes, M. (eds) (1981) *Women and Mental Health*, New York: Basic Books.

Nairne, K. and Smith, G. (1984) *Dealing with Depression*, London: Women's Press.

Penfold, P.S. and Walker, G.A. (1984) *Women and the Psychiatric Paradox*, Milton Keynes: Open University Press.

Rohrbaugh, J.B. (1981) *Women: Psychology's Puzzle*, London: Abacus.

Sanders, D. (1984) *Women and Depression*, London: Sheldon Press.

Scarf, M. (1981) *Unfinished Business*, London: Fontana.

Welburn, V. (1980) *Postnatal Depression*, Glasgow: Fontana.

For some useful books on *ethnic minority women* see:

Bryan, B., Dadzie, S. and Scafe, S. (1985) *The Heart of the Race. Black Women's Lives in Britain*, London: Virago Press.

Phizacklea, A. (ed.) (1983) *One Way Ticket. Migration and Female Labour*, London: Routledge and Kegan Paul.

Transcultural Psychiatry Society (1984) *Women: Cultural Perspectives*, Conference Report.

Wilson, A. (1978) *Finding a Voice: Asian Women in Britain*, London: Virago Press.

4 Sexism, Feminism and Social Work Practice

In this chapter we shall see that, unfortunately, social workers do not always succeed in adequately helping depressed women. This can in large part be attributed to the sexist ideology of social work and to the patriarchal nature of social work organizations. For these factors affect not only those working within the system, but also, and more crucially perhaps, they affect the actual practice of social work and the provision of services to clients. A feminist perspective can provide an antidote to current sex-biased theories, policies and procedures, and can form a useful framework from which to develop a more effective social work practice. In this chapter we thus begin by exploring how social workers fail in, or are constrained from, helping women in general, and depressed women in particular. Some ways in which a feminist perspective can help social workers to recognize and overcome these constraints are then considered.

Sexism and social work

We have already seen that psychosocial and sociostructural factors greatly contribute to women's vulnerability to depression. The implication of this is that such factors need to be taken into account when helping women to overcome depression. Unfortunately, however, social workers, like their medical colleagues, do not always address these factors. For, although social workers are generally concerned with social problems such as poverty and poor housing, they often do not fully appreciate how these problems interact with and affect emotional states and behaviour. Their concerns seem to remain either with social conditions *or* with intrapsychic difficulties, but the relationship between these factors is rarely addressed. Social workers, like other professionals, tend to individualize and depoliticize problems (Jones 1983). The interests of depressed women are not served by these means, nor by the tendencies of many social workers to blame women for family 'failure', to view them in sex-stereotypical ways (Brown and Hellinger

1975; Dailey 1980), or to disregard the gender disadvantage experienced by women.

There are a number of reasons why social workers, even female social workers, may continue to adhere to sexist values or may, unwittingly perhaps, oppress women. One reason may be the traditional and sex-biased perspective on the position of women that is clearly expressed in the literature of social work. A survey by Waller (1976) of some social work texts, confirmed that women are generally presented in sex-stereotypical ways. That is, they are consistently viewed only in terms of their domestic and servicing roles and are presumed to be passive, compliant and dependent. Women are also frequently expected to suppress their own needs for the good of the family as a whole. Further, female clients are usually considered inadequate, or labelled as 'problems' if they are perceived as being insufficiently able to fulfil nurturing roles. Whilst such stereotyping may possibly be less evident in the most recent social work literature, the gender disadvantage suffered by women is still not usually commented on.

In addition, most social work courses continue to promote a sexist ideology, partly through their often uncritical acceptance of gender roles, and partly through their failure to acknowledge or discuss issues, theories, policies and practices in terms of their effects on women. For example, the nuclear family is usually portrayed as fundamentally good, and of equal benefit to all parties. The significant effects of gender differences on life circumstances remains relatively unexplored in the social work field. Thus, both the social work literature and CQSW courses fail to offer theories and guidelines for practice that take into account the real needs and position of women.

Social workers may also tend to adhere to sexist attitudes because social work organizations are themselves patriarchal in structure and outlook. Women in SSDs tend to occupy inferior positions despite the fact that they are usually numerically stronger and generally better qualified than their male counterparts (Froggatt 1983). Women tend to be debarred from promotion to senior positions because of the existence of discriminatory employment practices. The shortage of child-care provision, the inflexibility of working hours and lack of part-time work at higher levels all still serve to keep women in the lower grade posts. Moreover, male dominated selection committees appear to favour the appointment of men to management positions (Popplestone 1980). The very existence of this power imbalance between men and women in social work organizations is likely to foster sexist attitudes and practices amongst the social workers working within them.

Social workers who do wish to address the needs of women, depressed or otherwise, are likely to be constrained by the sexist workings of the organizations that employ them. By virtue of their positions of power, men make the major decisions that affect the lives of clients as well as workers. They decide on such matters as the allocation of resources, including social work time and support, and largely determine both who becomes a social work client and what methods of intervention are used in practice. The oppression of women is unlikely to be taken into account in such decisions, resulting in sex-biased policies and practices. This may mean that a home help or day nursery place is less likely to be offered to a single mother than a single father; that a woman caring for her husband is less likely to be offered social work support than a man caring for his wife; and that in-depth casework with a depressed woman, or the running of a women's assertiveness group, may not be considered appropriate use of social work time.

The suffering of 'mentally ill' people is also often largely discounted by the policy-makers within SSDs. People with mental health problems have always been considered a low priority for social work assistance (DHSS 1978, Fisher *et al* 1984). This is partly because of the relative lack of legislation designed to meet their needs, but also, and more importantly, because of the values of the managers within SSDs. They do not seem to consider these people when determining what areas of non-statutory work to undertake, or when allocating funds for the provision of resources.

Social workers are also likely to be constrained from meeting the needs of depressed women by forces outside of their own organizations. For instance, many of the values enshrined in the welfare state negatively affect or discriminate against women. As Wilson (1977, 1983) has convincingly demonstrated, the welfare state both embraces and promulgates patriarchal relations and values. Legislation, social policy and the provision of services are all based on a traditional view of women and their duties. This view is reflected in much social security legislation, which still reinforces the economic dependency of women on men, and in the state's failure to make adequate provision for children, particularly those under five. Yet, despite its evident sex-bias, the welfare state provides many valuable services. However, the current financial restraints have led to a decline in service provision. This may well cause social workers to feel frustrated about not always being able to meet women's needs in practical and emotional ways. The shortage of all kinds of resources, from welfare benefits to houses and social facilities, means that women are often forced to remain in situations that are depressing and oppressing them. The increasing amount of time that social workers need to spend in attaining scarce resources and in dealing with bureaucratic procedures may also mean that there is less time for face-to-face therapeutic work.

As agents of the welfare state then, social workers, particularly those in SSDs, may find that they are in a position of shoring up a traditional view of women's duties whilst neglecting important areas of need.

Workers who try to respond to the sexism inherent in social work and specifically address the needs of women, may be viewed unfavourably. Feminist workers may be labelled as political extremists and exposed to the challenge of bias. Accusations might be made that 'because we fight for women's rights we cannot make "objective" assessments about women', or that 'we are rebelling against our own sexuality, acting out our fantasies through women, and forcing women to conform to our beliefs and values' (Birmingham Women and Social Work Group 1985, p.133). Feminist workers may well feel frustrated and isolated in their workplaces, as well as constrained by official policy and bureaucracy. Adopting a feminist perspective in a patriarchal environment does not make life easy. Given this situation, feminist workers would do well to begin by devising strategies for their own preservation. They might, for instance, consider joining a group of other like-minded people in their own or allied professions, where experiences can be shared and strength and support gained. Such groups might also have a consciousness-raising and campaigning element. Through collective action workers can attempt to combat the oppressive attitudes and practices of their departments and instigate the changes that are required to make them more responsive to the needs of women and all people with mental health problems. 'Women and Social Work' groups have already been established in some parts of Britain precisely for these purposes.

The contribution of feminism to social work practice

Working within a state agency clearly creates tensions for feminist social workers. Apart from the problems already discussed, feminist ideals of working cooperatively with colleagues and clients obviously end up being sacrificed to some extent. Yet there is still scope for alternative ways of working. Social workers do have some autonomy over the quantity and type of work they undertake, and the methods and styles of work they utilise in practice. They need to exploit this autonomy to meet the needs of women and develop additional ways of working with them. We shall now see how social workers can build on feminist theory to formulate a more comprehensive and expedient social work practice for the benefit of women in general and depressed female clients in particular. Feminism is the chosen approach because it addresses, rather than ignores, the external and internal factors that oppress women. It acknowledges that personal and political processes are inextricably linked and that we live in an unjust, male-dominated society.

In Chapters 2 and 3 it was shown that depression in women could be largely attributed to their roles in society and to the social conditions in which they live, as well as to the ways that they have learned to be and act as females. A feminist social work practice based on these conclusions will therefore aim to create changes on a sociostructural level as well as on an individual one. Social work built on feminism, however, cannot simply be taken on board and applied. It is largely made possible by a commitment to change which is motivated by the fact that workers, as well as clients, suffer from patriarchal oppression.

On a structural level, feminist social workers could work collectively to try and achieve change. They might attempt to ensure, for instance, that the needs and interests of women are not ignored and that the already existing discrimination against them is not further compounded by sex-biased practices and services. To this end, social workers might alert policy-makers and managers to the deleterious effects on women of their decisions and strategies. Actions such as writing letters and presenting reports could be directed at a local as well as national level, within SSDs and outside them. Workers could, for instance, draw the attention of the social work management to the additional burdens community care and fostering policies tend to place on women; put pressure on housing departments to provide better facilities for children; or campaign against proposed cuts in social security benefits. Feminist social workers should consider allying themselves with other agencies, whether statutory or voluntary (including those within the women's movement) to achieve desired changes.

Feminist workers might also want to develop innovative projects in the community, to create alternatives and empower groups of women. For example, they might set up housing or welfare rights surgeries, help open a drop-in counselling service, run assertiveness training groups, or initiate self-help groups for carers. Such initiatives may play a part in preventing or alleviating depression. To do these things social workers might need to join with feminist community workers or those working in the voluntary sector.

When working directly with clients, feminist workers will be concerned with empowering women to see and act on choices beyond those prescribed by the sexist social order. Depressed women in particular will need to be helped to consider alternative modes of being, reject their negative self-images and cease colluding with their own oppression.

A feminist worker would obviously not dispense with a multi-faceted assessment of each client simply because she is also concerned with the damaging effects of sexism. For a feminist perspective does not replace all knowledge of relevant theory, research and skills gained through general social work experience. Rather, it adds to and enhances them, and brings them up to date where the situation of women is concerned. A feminist consciousness brings a special sensitivity to, and understanding of, the kinds of problems contemporary women face. It means a heightened awareness of the psychological effects of social conditioning, sex roles and women's second-class status. Yet, a feminist perspective does not mean that women clients will be forced to be feminist themselves, or that they will be used, as has been suggested, as 'vehicles for the fall of patriarchy' (McQuaker and Specht 1982). What it does mean is that workers may draw on women clients' own experiences of oppression and depression to help them to understand the extent to which their problems may be the result of a sexist social structure. For women are usually only too well aware of being oppressed, even if they do not couch it in such terms.

Like other workers, feminists need to strive to take into consideration the oppression of all groups. For example, they should be sensitive to the needs of ethnic minority women, and avoid using methods that may be inappropriate to them. White workers should avoid imposing white feminist ideals upon black women. In dealing with women from communities with which they have had little experience, workers could seek advice about how best to help, or refer cases to those better equipped to deal with them. Social workers should not be afraid to admit their limitations in this and other respects.

In the following chapters we shall discuss some ways in which social workers can build on feminist theory to develop a range of methods to help depressed women. These methods are designed to empower women to act in ways denied them by the adherence to sex-stereotyped roles. They should also help women to increase the range of available options and life-chances and assist them in working through their sexist conditioning. Social workers should aim to be cognizant of a variety of approaches for helping women so that they and their clients can choose which therapeutic methods to use according to preference and need. The techniques discussed in this book are not of course the only appropriate means of meeting the needs of depressed women, but it is hoped that they will provide some useful ideas for social work practice.

Summary

In this chapter we have seen that the needs of women in general, and depressed women in particular, often fail to be addressed or attended to by the social work profession. This can largely be attributed to the following: (i) the sexist attitudes, values and practices of many social workers; (ii) the sexist nature of social work ideology; (iii) the inadequacy of theories for social work practice in relation to women; and (iv) the patriarchal nature of social work organizations and sex-biased social policy. While all these factors may act as constraints on social workers who do wish to meet the needs of depressed women, many of them can be overcome. It has been suggested that social workers may best be able to help depressed women by utilising a feminist perspective in their practice. This means bringing a special awareness and understanding to problems that women face. Feminist practice also involves working to achieve change on a societal, as well as personal and inter-

personal level. Feminist social workers may need to develop
new skills appropriate to these tasks.

Further reading

The Birmingham Women and Social Work Group (1985)
'Women and Social Work in Birmingham', in E. Brook, and
A. Davis (eds) *Women, The Family and Social Work*, London
and New York: Tavistock Publications.

Dailey, D.M. (1980) 'Are Social Workers Sexists? A
Replication,' *Social Work*, 25, 46–50.

Froggatt, A. (1983) 'Jobs for the Girls?,' *Social Work Today*,
14, 43, 7–9.

Hale, J. (1983) 'Feminism and Social Work Practice,' in B.
Jordan and N. Parton (eds) *The Political Dimensions of Social
Work*, Oxford: Blackwell.

Johnson, B.S. and Holton, C. (1976) 'Social Work and the
Women's Movement,' in B. Ross and S.K. Khinduka (eds)
Social work in practice, Washington: N.A.S.W.

Miles, J. (1981) 'Sexism in Social Work,' *Social Work Today*,
13, 1, 14–15.

Popplestone, R. (1980) 'Top Jobs for Women: Are the Cards
Stacked Against Them?,' *Social Work Today*, 12, 4, 12–15.

Richardson, D. (1981) 'Sexism in Social Work,' *Community
Care*, Nov. 5.

Wilson, E. (1977) *Women and the Welfare State*, London:
Tavistock Publications.

Wilson, E. (1980) 'Feminism and Social Work,' in M. Brake
and R. Bailey (eds) *Radical Social Work and Practice*,
London: Edward Arnold.

5 Feminist Casework

The caseloads of most social workers contain many depressed women. In addition to those who have sought help specifically for depression, there are many clients who are experiencing this problem but are seen by social workers for other reasons. Social workers need to be alert to any attempts by women to communicate their distress, and not be indifferent to their feelings because the case has been defined in such terms as 'child-care' or 'elderly'. Frequently it is the women who are the carers in these situations who present themselves to GPs with feelings of inadequacy, exhaustion, frustration and an inability to cope — in short, depression. But:

> five minutes with the GP whose time the patient has been taught is precious and 30 minutes with the social worker who limited the communication to the children's problems merely add to the sense of despair and alienation. (Ravetz 1982, p.14).

Thus direct social work intervention with women themselves is often required, desired and appropriate and may well be more efficacious than the drugs GPs prescribe. Indeed, constructive social work help at an early stage may avoid the need for subsequent referral to a GP or the psychiatric services.

A woman's depression obviously has consequences for her children and family (as indeed would a man's). A high correlation has been found to exist between maternal depression and emotional and behavioural disturbance in children (Wolff 1961; Richman 1977). Of course, if fathers or other people were more involved with child-care, the relationship between mothers and children would probably not be as crucial. Yet, the present reality is that the welfare of children is usually intimately connected with the functioning of their mothers. Thus Weissman *et al* (1972) suggest that early and intensive work with a depressed mother can 'facilitate major preventative work for the whole family.' However, casework in such instances is in danger of being oppressive. For instance, it might well induce guilt and affirm to a woman that she is solely responsible for the problems in her family. But it need not be so. Casework can be used to de-individualize problems and place women's roles in a structural context. Individual work can be a valuable and appropriate means of responding to the suffering of depressed women and used to enhance the quality of their lives. It allows them the often rare opportunity to have time to themselves in which they can explore and discuss problems and feelings.

Casework need not be the method of choice or the only approach used; it could be followed by family work, where for example men could be encouraged to share the child-care, or complemented or substituted by group work, where women can share problems together. Of course, casework does not preclude political or community action either.

The context: workers and clients
It is generally preferable for individual work with depressed women to be carried out by female workers. This is because they can act as potentially valuable role models to their clients and because they will share similar experiences of patriarchal oppression and sexism. Male workers on the other hand, will obviously not offer such advantages, and are also in danger of reproducing the power imbalance between men and women in society. However, the most important factor in practicing feminist casework is that workers are feminists themselves and that they have a deep understanding of women's issues and problems. A man who is non-sexist, subscribes to the aims of the women's movement and who is knowledgeable about women's psychology, would therefore be preferable as a worker to a woman who is sexist and anti-feminist in approach. The assumption of this book is, nevertheless, that it is female workers who will be working with female clients.

Whether male or female, it is important for workers continually to scrutinize their own motives, attitudes and behaviour. By doing so they are more likely to avoid imposing their own solutions, fantasies and desires onto clients, or making unreasonable demands of them. Good supervision is essential to facilitate such self analysis, as well as for preventing the common tendency of workers dealing with depressed people to become low or depressed themselves. If social workers are unable to attain supervision from within their own departments, they might consider joining or initiating feminist supervision or support groups.

The relationship between worker and client is of pivotal importance to the therapeutic process. Feminist workers consider that this relationship should be non-hierarchical whenever possible. This is particularly important for depressed women, who so easily fall into patterns of dependency and helplessness. However, workers need not deny the inevitable existence of some power imbalance between them and their clients, particularly in statutory cases where there may be a 'controlling' element. They could still use skills like setting limits and clarifying objectives (Llewelyn and Osborn 1983) but would avoid presenting themselves in the role of expert and refrain from using jargon or mystifying techniques. They would also share information and knowledge and discuss the possible effects of, and rationale for, a particular technique. As in all social work, the feminist worker would attempt to be empathetic and would offer warm, genuine support to the client and validate her feelings of depression and despair. Social workers might also share their own experiences and feelings if appropriate, to demystify themselves as omniscient, ever-coping professionals, and to diminish a client's feelings of inferiority and inadequacy. Common dilemmas of being a woman in a sexist society might also be discussed, although pertinent differences between the personal circumstances of the worker and client should not be ignored.

One means of lessening the power imbalance between workers and clients is to focus on the power that clients have in the therapeutic relationship. The client should be treated as essentially competent, as the one who knows best about her own feelings, thoughts and needs. A woman can learn to become less helpless and more independent if she is encouraged to take responsibility for herself, to take charge of her life and be aware of the processes by which she may be allowing others to have power over her. Such learning can begin in the context of the worker–client relationship and then be generalized to include other relationships.

Since women clients often have very little confidence in their own abilities, and may always expect others to assume control, workers need to remain continually sensitive to the ways in which they might begin to exploit their own authority and take control of the situation. Further, workers should always try to highlight and draw out the strengths and power of their clients, and foster women's own inherent ability to heal or change themselves. Drawing up contracts, where both individuals outline goals to be achieved, might be a useful means of ensuring that power is distributed more equally and that clients take responsibility for change. Using open files, where clients share in the writing of their own reports, might also be beneficial.

Shared power does not preclude workers being role models for clients. While workers might be willing to expose their weaknesses, they should also, ideally, be androgynous and assertive. They would thereby be demonstrating a woman's ability to take charge of her life and to succeed at a variety of endeavours. By having the opportunity to identify with a woman who does not share such a hopeless and helpless perception of the world, depressed clients may also be helped to see possibilities for change.

Most social workers do not have the time or skills to do long-term intensive psychotherapeutic work. They might therefore aim to keep the worker–client relationship as short as possible, although with the proviso of re-referral when necessary. This should ensure that the work is goal-oriented and has a specific purpose and direction. Short-term work also means that clients do not become too dependent upon something that will not always be available. Further, it reduces the risks of perpetuating a depressed client's perceived inability to help herself. Workers could thus be continually encouraging clients to build up their own support systems, introducing them, if appropriate, to self-help and other groups in the community. Specific self-help exercises and homework assignments or tasks that can be practiced without the aid of a worker might also be recommended. In some cases, books and other literature may provide useful sources of information to clients (see, for example, Rainwater 1981, McNeill Taylor 1983, Rowe 1983, Nairne and Smith 1984, Sanders 1984, Curran & Golombok 1985).

Strategies for overcoming depression
The points raised in Chapters 1 to 3 should aid social workers in assessing the reasons for a woman's depression and what is maintaining it. Assessment is likely to be an ongoing process between worker and client. What is revealed should determine the methods to be used to help clients and the particular

emphasis and nature of the work. While the specific causes and
precipitating events will be different in each instance, there are
some core features of women's depression which occur in most
cases. We shall thus address the similarities and the common
feelings experienced by depressed women to suggest ways in
which workers operating from a feminist perspective might
help these clients. The focus remains on fairly pragmatic ways
of helping. Issues associated with more intensive psychodynamic work, such as those connected with the subconscious,
or transference and counter-transference are not dealt with
here. Workers who are interested in these aspects, and feminist
psychotherapy generally, are referred to Eichenbaum and
Orbach (1982 and 1985). It is acknowledged that long-term
psychotherapy will sometimes be warranted for depressed
people. (This is discussed in Arieti and Bemporad 1978). But
for many women whom social workers come across, particularly
those in the community, the following strategies, incorporated
into a sympathetic casework approach, can go a long way in
helping to alleviate depression.

Practical assistance

As all good social workers, feminist practitioners should have a
thorough working knowledge of housing and welfare rights and
certain legal matters and should ensure that their clients receive
all the benefits they are entitled to. They might also share this
knowledge, encouraging women to take up issues themselves,
either on their own or with others. Social workers might recommend, for example, that women join or start claimants' unions
or tenants' groups with social work support as necessary.

Workers also need to be acquainted with, and know how to
gain access to, the various resources and groups available in the
community. They should be prepared to make full use of any
local authority services (for example, day nurseries, respite care
facilities, home helps, hostels) as well as those established by the
voluntary sector and the women's movement. They need to be
aware of how these services are provided so as to avoid, where
possible, those that are patriarchal and in danger of reinforcing
such feelings as female inferiority and helplessness. Ideally
clients should be able to select those services that are most
appropriate to them. For example, they might be offered a
choice between a local authority day nursery, run on traditional
lines, and a community nursery, where parents are involved in

the management and running of the service. It has to be acknowledged, however, that in many areas such alternatives will not be available and clients may be lucky to get access to any resource at all.

Reframing the situation

A feminist worker would not interpret depression as an individual pathological reaction, but view it as a possibly appropriate response to a probably unfair and oppressive situation. A depressed woman's feelings could then be acknowledged and validated as acceptable and clients would be encouraged to talk about them freely. The worker would align with the client in attempting to understand, and come to grips with the specific causes and meaning of her depression.

Taking the view that a woman may be struggling against adverse conditions, a worker could acknowledge and discuss the difficulties the client has come up against, for example, in rearing young children alone and in isolation. She might recognize that motherhood may be a joyous and wonderful experience, but that often it 'becomes a prison that warps the souls and minds of women when imposed as a 24-hour a day job' (Stevens 1971, p.13). The nuclear family in its present form need not be advocated as the only or 'natural' way in which to raise children, but acknowledged as something which reproduces and reinforces patriarchal power relations. The worker, then, stresses the client's positive achievements and her demanding roles, rather than viewing her as having failed to perform her 'natural' functions in life. In focusing on women's strengths and resources, workers can discover what can be built upon and utilised by clients to help themselves.

Workers could also draw out the commonality of clients' experiences with those of so many women, not as a means of invalidating them, but in order to break down their feelings of 'madness', guilt and isolation, and to promote a sense of unity with others of their sex.

Greater self-confidence, increased self-esteem and possibly a modification of any excessive expectations of self should soon begin to develop from workers adopting this stance.

Examining the external–internal dynamic

Depressed women typically blame themselves for problems they encounter and feel guilty and inadequate if their behaviour deviates from social expectations. For instance, women often feel it is all their fault if their husbands are abusive towards them, if their house is not perfectly clean and tidy, or if they do not succeed in getting a job. It is thus essential to help them recognize how they may have internalized societal prescriptions and how external and environmental factors can influence their lives and behaviour.

Worker and client could discuss how attitudes, values and practices towards women have affected, and are affecting them in ways which cause distress. For example, they could explore how discriminatory employment practices might be preventing a woman getting the promotion she deserves; how her parenting and schooling prepared her for subordinate and passive behaviour, so that she finds it difficult to break out of negative self-defeating patterns; how stereotyped images of feminine beauty may be contributing to her negative body-image and feelings of inferiority; or how a woman's sense of inadequacy and of being a 'bad' mother is connected with how she has been conditioned to believe a mother 'ought' to be. Worker and client can then discusss whether adherence to such attitudes and values is still appropriate or if they may be discarded in the interests of mental health. Once women are aware of their conditioning they are often motivated to give up roles and behaviours that are causing stress or distress. Helping them to differentiate who they are from the roles they are fulfilling and shifting some of the responsibility for 'failure' away from them, should serve to increase their self-esteem and confidence and reduce feelings of guilt.

Women are not merely victims of circumstances or sex-role stereotyping however. They need to be helped to distinguish between which behaviours are the result of internalized societal prescriptions, which are in response to current social pressures and which are more the consequence of personal or inter-personal difficulties. Women should then be encouraged to accept responsibility for changing whatever they need to and can.

Generating alternatives
Once social workers have assisted women to recognize and locate which particular areas of their lives or ways of behaving can be changed, they can help them to recognize what choices and alternatives are open to them. Workers might begin by encouraging clients to think about how they can act in their *own*

interests, rather than doing what they think they ought to or what brings approval. If women have lost touch with their own needs and desires, workers will firstly have to help them to differentiate what *they* want and think, from what others (husbands, mothers, children) want and think. Social workers can then encourage them to speculate about what they want for themselves. A useful technique here might be to suggest a woman fantasizes about what she would be doing in an ideal world, or list activities she would most like to engage in. She might then specify which changes she can make for herself and which she would like others to make for her. For example, a woman might decide that she wants to make more friends and that she wants her husband to do more child-care. Thus ideas can be generated about how women can gain pleasure in their lives, take responsibility for change and begin to overcome depression. They can then discuss with a worker how these ideas, however 'outrageous' or stereotypically 'unfeminine' might be put into practice. Any ideas for change can be prioritized and broken down into small easy steps so that one area can be chosen and targeted for immediate alternative action. This is important because depressed people typically set themselves unrealistic goals which ensure failure and hence self-recrimination. Just by identifying 'possibilities of acting, reacting, defining and influencing that do exist, the client will begin to realize that she need not feel bound or victimized' (Berlin 1976, p.494). Actually engaging in change should dispel overwhelming feelings of incompetence, apathy and helplessness. Change in one small area should be self-reinforcing, motivating the woman to alter other distressing aspects of her life. Any changes, however small, need to be rewarded by both worker and client. Depressed women in particular need to be encouraged to recognize, own and reward their achievements, rather than attributing them to luck or the actions of others.

Depressed housewives might decide that they could be helped by getting employment outside the home. They would obviously need to explore how realistic this is, what kind of jobs are available and if it would actually achieve the purpose of alleviating the depression. Workers would need to be sympathetic to a woman's difficulties in this area, such as any feelings of inadequacy about entering a male-dominated workplace or of guilt about leaving her children. They should obviously be prepared to help with practical arrangements where necessary.

Getting a job in times of high unemployment is not easy but, if achieved, may lead to increased self-esteem and confidence, and a feeling of being needed and valued. Furthermore, by earning her own money, a woman's dependency on others and any feelings of resentment at such dependency should diminish and a sense of self-satisfaction ensue.

Where women cannot find work or do not wish to do so, it is essential to make them feel valued in the role they currently fulfil. Whilst the restrictions of a dependent role may need to be acknowledged, this need not be done in a way that devalues the entirety of the role. Workers should be wary of reinforcing society's negative image of 'women's work'; they should be able to recognize and foster any potential for creativity, autonomy and competence within that work.

One area in which depressed women typically need help and want to change is in overcoming their isolation and loneliness. Often they have withdrawn from all social situations, believing that others share the low opinion that they have of themselves. Indeed, a poor self-image and negative state does conspire to alienate other people, thus perpetuating negative feelings and isolation. A worker could be helpful in breaking into this vicious circle by giving women the confidence to generate some social contacts. To help in this, workers might consider teaching their clients some (non-sexist) social skills (Trower *et al* 1978). They could also support and encourage women to become involved in a variety of community activities. They could, for instance, suggest a woman starts by joining a self-help group such as 'depressives anonymous', 'Gingerbread', or a mental health system 'survivors' group.

Feminist workers might encourage their female clients to develop friendships with other women. Some women may first need help to see that they do not need to despise or be in competition with others of their sex, but that they can learn to rely on them for the support they need. This is often necessary because a depressed woman's low self-esteem is frequently manifested in a low opinion, and even hatred of other women.

By developing friendships, interests and new activities that are meaningful to her, a woman should find that her depressed mood begins to lift. The broadening of horizons should also assist in developing her own identity and place previous goals and aspirations, such as being an 'ideal' wife or mother, into a new context. Women should begin to feel more in control of their own lives and less dependent on others for approval and feelings of self-worth.

Social workers need to remain aware that initiating change, particularly in non-traditional feminine fields will be risky and usually viewed with ambivalence by women. For women may be aware of the threat that their own personal changes may impose on others, and may fear a negative response from them. Indeed, a woman's move towards 'liberation' can be disruptive to family life and is frequently met with a great deal of resistance, and sometimes hostility. Women will need to talk through these concerns, weigh up the advantages and disadvantages to change and then choose to act in ways they see fit. Workers should support women through any periods of transition and disruption, preparing them for impasses and steps backward which are inevitable and not evidence of failure. They might help prepare women for their actions, and the reactions of others, by discussion and role-rehearsal. New skills and behaviours can be practised and tried out in the safety of the client–worker relationship.

When a woman finds it too difficult to effect change on her own it might at some stage be appropriate to involve her spouse and/or other family members in casework. Workers can act as mediators or enable change to take place in the family sphere by, for instance, helping spouses to recognize the value that outside interests and friendships can have in alleviating depression in their wives. A husband may be encouraged to help his wife by viewing her as a person in her own right, by allowing her to be more autonomous, and by encouraging her to be less dependent upon him. Men may be helped to overcome any feelings of resentment and jealousy at their wives' attempts at independence by learning to see that such behaviour need not be a threat or denial of the marital relationship. Workers might also help couples to renegotiate the family rules, roles and tasks so that family life becomes less oppressive to the woman. Where familial relationships are particularly problematic, however, more intensive marital or family therapy may be indicated. This can be useful after individual work has helped to alleviate the most distressing aspects of a woman's depression and contributed to raising her self-esteem. Readers interested in feminist couple or family therapy are referred to Rice and Rice 1977, Hare-Mustin 1978, Eichenbaum and Orbach 1982, 1984.

Encouraging nurturance, anger and grief

Feminist social workers should recognize and acknowledge women's need for love and nurturance as well as for autonomy and independence. We have seen how women have been socialized to believe that their primary function in life is to nurture others and that in their self-sacrificing role they may have lost a sense of their own needs and wishes. While in a state of deep depression, a woman may have relinquished the caring role to some extent, but she will doubtless be feeling guilty and be anxious to resume it. Workers may therefore first need to help women overcome their guilt and modify their expectations of nurturing others, and then encourage them to nurture and love themselves. Depressed women need to be continually reminded that they have needs and rights of their own, distinct from those of others and that sometimes it would be best if they put their own needs first. Workers might assist women in examining instances where they have acceded to the demands of others against their own interests and discuss how they could have done otherwise.

Depressed women often neglect themselves in very basic ways, such as by not eating or sleeping sufficiently, and feel that they are unworthy of any attention, even from themselves. Workers must help them to restore a sense of their own worth and encourage them to take care of themselves and their bodies. They might, for example, help a woman plan a daily routine with this in mind, or suggest she thinks about what she likes about herself, rather than what she hates, or encourage her to think of ways she can regularly treat herself to things she enjoys. Depressed women also need to generate an awareness of how others can nurture them, and recognize that it is valid to be cared for, as well as to care. They need to be able to ask clearly for what they want from others, which may be difficult. The development of assertiveness skills may help clients in this respect. Taking responsibility for themselves in this way can engender an increased sense of mastery and heighten satisfaction in relationships with others. Women who can also learn to love themselves will be less reliant on others for approval and have a more sturdy sense of self.

Depressed women might be better able to like themselves if they expressed some of the anger and rage that is so often turned inward and tied up in self-hate. Because women have been socialized to believe that anger is inappropriate for them, they may regard the expression of all negative feelings as being in total conflict with their self-image, and fear that it will jeopardise their reserves of love and approval. Reassurance is thus needed that such feelings are reasonable, appropriate and even healthy. A safe and secure environment is an essential pre-requisite for female clients to vent these emotions. Gestalt and other exercises may be useful in encouraging the expression of such feelings in the safety of the worker–client relationship (see Ernst and Goodison 1981 for examples), while discussion, behavioural rehearsal and role playing might assist women in expressing anger to other people. Women might also be pre-pared by these means for the reactions of others to their new-found ways of relating.

Social workers might also need to encourage women to express their distress and hurt through tears and other means. While many depressed women spend a good deal of time crying, others barely allow themselves to shed a single tear. Weeping in front of a sympathetic other who can tolerate and contain pain and suffering can be a very therapeutic experience and a sign that healing is taking place. Women may also need to be given explicit permission to mourn for a loss, past or present, whether the loss be youth, looks, independence, a baby, a parent in childhood or whatever. Depression is often associated with a failure to grieve an important loss earlier in life and the social worker might consider engaging a woman in some grief therapy if appropriate. Much has been written about grief and bereavement work and the reader is referred to two excellent books on the subject by Tatelbaum (1980) and Worden (1983).

Case examples

1. Jane M. was referred to the SSD by a health visitor who was concerned about the care of her two year old child and the mounting debts in the home. Jane was labelled an 'in-adequate mum'.

   The social worker visited to find Jane depressed, anxious and miserable. She had moved recently to the estate after the break-down of her marriage and found herself lonely and cut off from friends and family. She felt overwhelmed by the financial problems and unable to cope on her own with her daughter, Mandy. The worker noticed that Mandy seemed rather under-stimulated but was otherwise well cared for. She tried to offer some hope to Jane and encouraged her to see that as a single-parent with a young child she was battling against many odds, but that with some help from the worker, they could together find ways in which her burden might be eased. A contract for an initial ten sessions was made between them (later extended), with the financial difficulties targeted as the most pressing issue to be dealt with.

The worker first ensured that Jane was in receipt of all the benefits she was entitled to and then helped her to work out more practical ways of budgeting and paying bills. The worker helped Jane to see that her financial difficulties arose not so much from her own inability to cope, but rather from the fact that she had to manage on a very meagre income. Jane admitted to feeling inadequate about her ability to cope with practical issues as well as about her role as a parent. She felt guilty about not being a 'good enough' mother and about Mandy not having two parents around. The worker tried to encourage Jane to see that her sense of inadequacy was partly a result of her unrealistically high expectations of what mothers should do and be like, that she had internalized from the wider society. The worker praised her for managing as well as she had and focused on her strengths, rather than her weaknesses. She also assured Jane that she was not alone with her difficulties and that many women understandably found it hard to cope with a young child without support and with few financial resources.

To help Jane overcome her sense of isolation and her child-care problems the worker encouraged her to join a variety of groups in the community. Jane felt fearful initially and anxious about meeting new people, but after some support and encouragement she did join a couple of mother and toddler groups. Mandy thus gained an opportunity to play with other children and Jane began to develop some contacts. After a few weeks she made a friend with whom she could go to the local Gingerbread club. Jane began to feel less depressed as she became involved in activities outside the home and made some friends. As a result, her relationship with Mandy also improved.

There were still times when Jane felt too miserable to go out, was apathetic and didn't care for herself properly. The worker tried to help her to plan and structure her days in advance, so that she did not wake up with a blank day to face. Together they worked out ways of keeping Mandy and herself amused and they planned routines for meals, exercise and sleep. With the worker's help Jane also wrote a list of ways she could treat herself when she felt low and depressed. Jane's list included having a long bubble bath, listening to a record loudly and eating a cream cake. With the worker's permission to indulge herself, Jane felt less guilty about doing so, and found herself increasingly able to engage in pleasurable activities which either forestalled, or lifted a low mood.

Jane spent a number of sessions talking about her marriage and relationship with her husband, Jon. The worker tried to help her work through her loss and grief, and encouraged her to express her anger and sadness about the situation, as well as her feelings of helplessness and inadequacy about being a woman on her own. The worker acknowledged her need for support and dependency whilst also encouraging her to develop the independent, adventurous side to her character.

After a few months Jane began to feel more valued as a person and more coping. She felt sufficiently confident to get a part-time job at a local shop and child-minding was arranged for Mandy. It was agreed to withdraw social work support, but Jane felt that she would be able to contact the worker again if necessary.

2. Mrs Cook, who was suffering from senile dementia, was referred to the SSD for respite care in part three (elderly persons) accommodation. When the social worker visited her home she found Mrs Cook's daughter, Mrs Bea, to be agitated and upset and in her own words, 'at the end of my tether with my mother'. Mrs Bea admitted that she had felt increasingly depressed and non-coping over the last few months. The social worker felt that she needed help in her own right and Mrs Bea agreed that she could benefit from time to talk things over with someone not involved in the situation. A contract for an initial five sessions was made between them.

Mrs Bea looked after her forgetful, 75 year old mother day in and day out, almost single-handed, and had been doing so for the last ten years. Mr Bea was at work all day

and their children had left home. The situation at the Bea
household had been deteriorating with Mrs Cook's increasing senility, leaving everyone feeling tense and irritable. Mrs Cook could no longer fend for herself, be left in
the house alone or engage in meaningful conversation. Mrs
Bea was consequently on the point of giving up her job of
six hours a week to attend to her mother absolutely full-
time. Although she felt that her job was the only thing that
kept her going, Mrs Bea felt that her primary allegiance and
responsibility must be to her mother. Nevertheless, she
naturally felt rather reluctant and resentful about giving up
her only independent activity, yet guilty about having those
feelings. In addition, Mrs Bea felt very hesitant about
placing her mother in an elderly persons home (EPH) even
for one week, while she went on holiday with her husband.
At the same time, Mrs Bea knew that she badly needed a
holiday otherwise she would 'crack' under the pressure.
Furthermore, she had had very little time alone with her
husband for a number of years and this was putting the
marital relationship under considerable strain.

With the worker, Mrs Bea talked through these feelings,
plus her guilt about not being a 'good enough' daughter;
her hatred of old people's homes, and her fear that she herself was going 'mad'. The worker helped Mrs Bea to see
that her image of a 'good daughter', was a most unrealistic
ideal, instilled in her through her upbringing in a
patriarchal society; a society which refused to seriously acknowledge both the needs of women as people in their own
right and the needs of elderly persons. Mrs Bea came to see
that the values she had internalized were oppressing her
and causing her to be depressed and that her reactions were
normal rather than pathological. The worker encouraged
Mrs Bea to attend to her own needs and to see that she had
a duty to herself as well as to her mother. She helped Mrs
Bea to see that working a few hours a week and having a
holiday were her rights and that her guilt was needless, but
understandable. Mrs Bea soon came to acknowledge that
for the sake of her own sanity she would have to begin to
share the caring of her mother. She also acknowledged,
what she already knew deep down, that it was because she
was a woman that she was in that situation at all. For Mrs
Bea admitted to the worker that she had two brothers who

had always refused to take any responsibility for their mother, and who, moreover, never seemed to feel guilty about it. Mrs Bea admitted to colluding in the situation by not encouraging the men to share the caring. She now tried to swallow her anger about it all. But the worker encouraged her to express the rage, hurt and resentment that she felt towards her brothers, as well as the similar, but more repressed feelings towards her mother.

After five sessions Mrs Bea and the worker agreed to the following:

1. A home help would be found to look after Mrs Cook on the two mornings Mrs Bea went to work, plus one other afternoon in which Mrs Bea could have time for herself.
2. Mrs Bea, Mrs Cook and the worker would visit some EPHs with a view to arranging respite care.
3. A meeting would be called between Mrs Bea, her two brothers and their families, plus the worker, in order to discuss the situation and to encourage the men to take more responsibility for their mother.

After visiting some EPHs Mrs Bea felt much relieved, for while they were neither particularly cheerful nor luxurious, they were not the dreadful places she had imagined them to be. She felt her mother would be well looked after and could cope for one week.

As a result of the family meeting, Mrs Bea and her two brothers agreed to take care of their mother on alternate Sundays, thus allowing Mrs Bea to have some Sundays free. The brothers also fully supported their mother going into an EPH for a week and agreed to visit her regularly.

Mrs Bea kept her job and went on her week's holiday. On her return, seeing that her mother was quite happy, she asked the worker to arrange respite care on a regular basis. At the worker's suggestion Mrs Bea also joined SEMI — a self-help group for carers, where she could gain ongoing support.

Summary

We have seen that a feminist approach to casework implies that it is often helpful to encourage depressed women to express anger and grief, develop their own potential and determine and pursue what they want for themselves. Feminist casework also means helping depressed women to see that their distress may be a natural reaction to a difficult and oppressive situation, and that the depression may be connected with their roles as women in a patriarchal society. Feminist workers could try to help women to understand the relationship between internal and external oppression, and to acknowledge the impact of social and environmental factors on their lives. At the same time, workers should encourage women to take responsibility for changing whatever they can.

Feminist casework is carried out in the context of non-hierarchical relationships between workers and clients, where clients are treated as competent and encouraged to take charge of their own growth.

It is necessary for any attempts to achieve change on an individual level to be placed in a structural context. Social workers should remember that there are limits to personal change and be aware of constraints imposed by society and often by a woman's family. If these constraints are not recognized workers may 'blame the victim' and cause clients to label themselves as inadequate and personal failures. Also, women need to be prepared for the conflicting responses they may encounter if they break out of stereotypical patterns. With these points in mind we shall now turn to look at a specific method — cognitive therapy — that can be useful to depressed women and fruitfully incorporated into a feminist perspective.

Further Reading

Berlin, S. (1976) 'Better Work with Women Clients,' *Social Work*, 21, 6, 492–7.

Brook, E. and Davis, A. (eds) (1985) *Women, The Family and Social Work*, London: Tavistock Publications.

Eichenbaum, L. and Orbach, S. (1982) *Outside In Inside Out*, Harmondsworth: Penguin.

Eichenbaum, L. and Orbach, S. (1985) *Understanding Women*, Harmondsworth: Penguin.

Hale, J. (1983) 'Feminism and Social Work Practice,' in B. Jordan and N. Parton (eds) *The Political Dimensions of Social Work*, Oxford: Blackwell.

Howell, E. and Bayes, M. (eds) (1981) *Women and Mental Health*, New York: Basic Books.

Llewelyn, S. and Osborn, K. (1983) 'Women as Clients and Therapists,' in D. Pilgrim (ed.) *Psychology and Psychotherapy*, London: Routledge and Kegan Paul.

Mander, A.V. and Rush, A.K. (1974) *Feminism as Therapy*, New York and California: Random House/Bookworks.

Moskol, M.D. (1976) 'Feminist Theory and Casework Practice', in B. Ross and S.K. Khinduka (eds) *Social Work in Practice*, Washington: NASW.

Rawlings, E.I. and Carter, D.K. (eds) (1977) *Psychotherapy for Women*, Illinois: Thomas.

Ryan, J. (1983) *Feminism and Therapy*, London: Polytechnic of North London.

6 Cognitive Therapy

Cognitive therapy (CT) has been found to be a very effective method for helping to alleviate depression. Research indicates that the benefits of the therapy can begin to be felt almost immediately and that these gains can be maintained over time (Rush *et al* 1977; Kovacs *et al* 1981; Teasdale and Fennel 1982). However, CT may not always be sufficient in itself to help depressed women, for as we have seen already, depression is generally more than the result of cognitive distortions. Nevertheless it can be usefully incorporated into feminist oriented individual work and used with some of the strategies outlined in Chapter 5. Although CT is as yet rarely used by social workers, there is no reason why it should not become part of their repertoire of skills. It is a straightforward approach that should be no harder to learn than behaviour modification, which is already a well established part of social work training and practice.

In Chapter 2 the basic tenets of cognitive theory were outlined. To recapitulate, the theory asserts that emotional reactions result from cognitions or statements people make to themselves regarding what they perceive to be reality. Thoughts thus mediate between events and emotional responses. Depression follows from exclusively negative and pessimistic thinking about the self, the world and the future. The depressed person has absolute faith in her negative beliefs and the resulting depression and/or somatic symptoms appear to her to be confirmation of the validity of these beliefs. The individual is thus involved in a self-perpetuating closed system where she goes 'round and round, deeper into the spiral of depression' (Burns and Beck 1978, p.111).

Cognitive theory interprets as causal what other theories regard merely as symptoms of depression. Yet there is little conclusive evidence that distorted cognitions do actually *cause* depression. If the experience of being depressed leads one to think negatively, rather than vice versa, the implications for treatment may be different. Nevertheless, the undoubted significance of negative and distorted thoughts in the maintenance of depression, suggests that CT is likely to be useful, at least in curbing depression.

Cognitive therapists have found that the distortions involved in the cognitions of depressed persons can be unlearned. The aim of the therapy is thus to assist individuals in changing their negative and depressogenic attitudes towards themselves and their environments. CT can be used to help depressed women to challenge their negative self-attributions, modify their un-realistic expectations and break out of self-defeating sex-stereo-typical patterns. As Beck and Greenberg (1974) comment, CT can help women to recognize cultural prejudices and negative evaluations of women, for what they are — 'attitudes that may rule masses of people, but need in no way affect an individual's estimate of her own worth' (p.130).

This is what some women have said about how their thoughts have caused, or played a part in their depression:

I really thought it was all my fault — that I wasn't a good enough wife and mother and that I should try harder ... I completely blamed myself for getting in that situation. He made me feel guilty and wrong and I accepted it all. Believing all that made me feel really depressed.

Because I thought my parents didn't love me I thought everyone else hated me as well. I stopped seeing my friends 'cause I thought they didn't want to see me and then I got more and more lonely. I isolated myself because I thought people hated me, and the more I isolated myself the more I believed that. So I got more and more depressed. But now that I'm happier I realize that I wasn't actually right.

Here is one woman's view about her thinking processes and how challenging them seemed to help:

When I'm depressed I talk a load of rubbish, it might be vital to me at the time, but it's usually impractical, illogical and everything's blown out of all proportion. My social worker is really good, because she listens to me and if she thinks I'm talking rubbish she tells me I am, whereas most people are frightened to do that. She makes me realize that what I'm saying is daft. I might rant and rave at the time, but deep down I know what I'm saying is a load of rubbish. It's good to rant and rave 'cause then it brings it all out, rather than it going round and round in your head ... she helps me to sort out the fact and fiction, because when you're depressed the paths between fact and fiction cross really easily. You're aware initially when you're doing it, but after a while the fiction becomes fact and you end up believing it ... When you're depressed you need someone to help you think straight, because you're so confused as to what's what.

In the following pages we shall look briefly at the principle techniques employed in CT. These are based mainly on the work of Aaron Beck and his colleagues, the chief proponents of the model (Beck 1976; Beck and Greenberg 1974; Burns and Beck 1978; Beck *et al* 1979).

The therapy

Cognitive therapy is a pragmatic, active approach, involving client and worker in a collaborative effort to combat depression. A time limit (usually 15–25 sessions) may be set to achieve desired goals, and specific problematic areas, such as social isolation or self-criticism, can be targeted for intervention. Since the various phenomena of depression (thoughts, feelings, behaviour and so on) are closely intertwined, change in any one area is likely to produce improvements in others. The focus of the approach is on the here and now, concerned with conscious, rather than unconscious, behaviour, thoughts and problems that are currently affecting the client. Cognitive therapists typically use a wide range of techniques to help clients (see Beck 1976), many of which overlap with behaviour therapy. The cognitive elements of the therapy are concentrated on here.

In the cognitive therapeutic process the worker assists the client to identify and modify maladaptive thoughts and assumptions, and then helps her to replace these negative views with more adaptive, less depression-inducing ones. We shall now elaborate on how this process is carried out.

Discovering and monitoring automatic thoughts

A primary CT technique consists of helping clients to recognise the negative self-statements or 'automatic thoughts' that lead to a lowering of mood. These thoughts are called 'automatic' because they arise rapidly, as if by reflex and most depressed people are barely aware of them. When they feel low or suddenly more depressed, they are not aware that a thought has intervened between a particular event and their lowered mood. However, a woman can train herself to increase her awareness of automatic thoughts by careful self-monitoring. The worker might suggest that as a homework assignment the client attempts to notice and record when she has a negative or self-critical thought or pictorial image, or makes self-denigrating statements. By this means the connection between thought, feeling and behaviour becomes apparent. The act of recording the negative thought may in itself prevent a lowering of mood, since it may make such thoughts seem less real or valid.

Example. A mother begins to notice that every time her child cries and is sick she thinks to herself 'I'm a useless mother and a terrible cook. The child must hate my food otherwise she wouldn't bring it up. If I wasn't such a bad mother she would at least stop crying.' These thoughts leave her feeling uncoping and depressed.

If a woman finds it difficult to 'thought-catch' on her own, the worker could suggest she tries within the sessions to imagine recent events she found distressing, or to role-play situations she found difficult, to see what thoughts come up.

Examination, evaluation and modification of thoughts
By exposing automatic thoughts and negative self-evaluations, client and worker are afforded the opportunity to examine, challenge and modify them. Depressed women typically accept their interpretations of reality at face value and remain convinced that their automatic thoughts are accurate and reasonable. So, the worker needs to help her client to distance herself from her thoughts, to view them critically and to assess whether they are realistic or justified. Sometimes clients will at this point need to be helped to make a distinction between thought and external 'reality'. They may need to be made aware that just because they think something it does not mean it is necessarily true. For example, a woman who thinks she is useless, inadequate and unattractive can be helped to realise that this is merely her own judgement, not a statement of an objective fact. A useful technique for helping women to distance themselves and reappraise the validity of their thoughts is a 'Daily Record

of Dysfunctional Thoughts' (see Figure 6.1) which the client can do as a homework assignment.

The worker could also help a depressed woman by drawing attention to ways in which she may misinterpret events or situations. There are a variety of different distorted cognitive responses that all people, but particularly depressed women tend to make. Some common types of distortion are as follows:

a) *Absolutist or dichotomous reasoning:* Everything is seen in all or nothing, black and white terms, e.g. 'If he leaves I might as well be dead'.
b) *Personalisation:* A person attributes all bad things to herself despite evidence to the contrary.
c) *Arbitrary inference:* Interpreting a single event as evidence of failure, rejection or unworthiness, without considering alternatives. E.g. 'Since my social worker is late she can't be interested in me'.
d) *Over-generalization:* Drawing broad generalizations and conclusions on the basis of a single or unrepresentative piece of evidence. E.g. 'As I didn't get this job I must be an inadequate person'.
e) *Magnification/minimisation:* Tending to exaggerate or minimize the significance of a particular event. E.g. 'I only came top in the exam because everyone else was ill-prepared'.
f) *Selective abstraction:* Focusing on a single detail rather than the whole context of the situation.

The worker can help her client to identify and challenge such distortions in her thinking. Together they can assess the likelihood of the validity of her thoughts and discuss alternative responses to situations. For instance, if a woman makes a statement like 'I never succeed at anything' after a single, isolated failure, the worker can help her to recognize such an over-generalization, by focusing on situations where she has succeeded. The woman could then modify her statement to one that reflects a more balanced view of her capabilities, such as 'I haven't succeeded on this occasion, although at other times I have, and I am often successful in other areas.' Learning to substitute alternative, more positive self-statements for negative ones in a variety of situations may help arrest the processes that lead to depression. By this means clients can prepare them-

Situation	Emotion(s)	Automatic thoughts	Rational response	Outcome
What were you doing or thinking about?	What do you feel?	What exactly were your thoughts?	What are your rational answers to the automatic thoughts?	1. How far do you now believe the automatic thoughts (0–100%)?
What was the event that led to the unpleasant emotion?	How bad was it (0–100)?	How far did you believe each of them (0–100%)?	How far do you believe each of them (0–100%)?	2. How do you feel? (0–100)
Teacher rang and asked me to come into school to discuss Jo's behaviour today.	Anxious, guilty and depressed 90	He must have done something really dreadful. That confirms what a bad mother I am. They'll get angry and blame me. 85%	It is probably just an isolated incident. They have never complained about him before so I can't be such a bad mother. They won't necessarily blame me for his behaviour. 95%	20% Relieved 60 Anxious 20
Boss criticised a piece of my work.	Upset and depressed 70	I can't do this job. I'm useless. 75%	That piece of work just wasn't as good as usual because I wasn't well when I did it. Overall I'm competent and good at the job. 95%	5% Upset 15

Figure 6.1 Daily record of dysfunctional thoughts

Source: Drawn and adapted from Beck *et al* 1979.

selves for occasions which may be anxiety or depression provoking.

Depressed women could be encouraged to test out their negative self-statements and thoughts in real-life situations. The approach to this would be experimental — the client is testing out her hypothesis in the field, not putting herself in a success/failure situation. Workers can prepare clients for such tasks by discussion and/or role-play. Frequently, assumptions are invalidated when they are empirically tested and the depressed person may find that her fantasies are worse than reality. One success in this area may encourage clients to be more adventurous in others and self-esteem should be raised. Furthermore, by carrying out a task the depressed person is stimulated into action and the likelihood of positive reinforcements is increased.

Example. Ms A says she thinks *all* her friends are bored with her and that none of them want anything more to do with her. She believes this 100 per cent and concludes that she is herself a boring and worthless person. On probing, the worker discovers that her client is basing her conclusions on the fact that two friends have not called on her in the past week, as they usually do. Worker and client decide how Ms A can find out if her belief is true. They agree that she will telephone two or three people, one friend whom she had expected to see and at least one other. She will ask them to come over for coffee at an arranged time. Worker and client role-play the situation and discuss what Ms A is likely to feel and what she is likely to conclude, from both affirmative and negative responses from others. The results are to be noted and brought back for discussion the following week.

When Ms A returns for her next appointment she feels much more positive about herself. She had ascertained that the friend whom she had expected to call on her had gone away suddenly and was still away. The other friend was pleased to be invited over and came at the arranged time.

From this exercise Ms A learned that her negative self-evaluations and self-talk were not always justified and could be reappraised.

By continually evaluating thoughts and experiences and subjecting perceptions to 'reality-testing', depressed women may gain greater insight into the processes by which they become distressed. With this knowledge they should be better equipped to meet new difficulties that arise, which may well serve to prevent further depressions.

Identification, examination and modification of primary assumptions

Peoples lives are often regulated and directed by deep seated assumptions and belief systems. In women, these are often related to sex-stereotypical themes and to what they have been socialized to believe are appropriate modes of behaviour for females. Some common assumptions held by women, particularly depressed women, are:

Women can only be successful if they are slim and beautiful;
Women should never get angry;
Women should be kind and selfless at all times and never hurt anyone;
You are only a real woman if you are married and have children;
To be happy I must be accepted and liked by all people at all times;
My value as a person depends on what others think of me.

Worker and client can together attempt to discover what a woman's 'rules for living' are and whether any of these may be causing distress and depression. The client can then make a more informed decision about whether she wants to continue to adhere to these rules or whether she would rather substitute them with other more appropriate and healthy ones. It might be helpful to list the advantages and disadvantages of adhering to particular beliefs or life-mandates, in order to clarify what may be lost and what gained by change. If there appear to be sufficient benefits a woman should feel motivated to change. The worker would then help the client to think of alternative ways of acting in various situations and support her through her attempts to adapt to new modes of being.

Example. Anne had been married to Bob for five years and had two children. Bob often hit her about, kept her enslaved in the house, and ensured that she did all the housework, cooking and child-care. He did not allow her to go out in the evening alone or to have friends in the house, so she had got progressively more isolated and lonely. Every time she began to do something against Bob's wishes she felt so guilty she couldn't continue with it. She was unhappy with the marriage, felt she didn't love Bob any more, but felt powerless to leave him. She was feeling increasingly depressed, hopeless and helpless.

Anne and the worker discussed how she was, like many women, emotionally and financially dependent upon a man whom she no longer had a good relationship with. Apart from the financial difficulties, they realized that Anne felt stuck with Bob because of certain assumptions and rules that were governing her life. These were:

i) Once you've made your bed you must lie on it forever.
ii) Children should have their father around.
iii) Women should serve others and not be selfish.
iv) Women who get beaten up deserve it.
v) Women always need to have a man to rely on.

Anne and the worker discussed how Anne was subject to patriarchal oppression which she had internalized. They went through each 'demand' to see what effect it had on her feelings and if she still felt it was valid and necessary to adhere to it. They discussed the costs and benefits of the traditional female role to see what Anne would lose if she gave up her role and left Bob, as part of her so much wanted to do. Anne saw that many of her internal demands were not even realized in the context of her present relationship and that in many ways she would be better off living apart from Bob. On reflection the costs and losses seemed to pale into insignificance. The worker supported her through her decision in practical and emotional ways.

The strategies of CT should be used sensitively and with flexibility. They may be usefully combined with behavioural methods, such as task assignments or social skills exercises when appropriate. However, as Beck *et al* (1979) have themselves pointed out, whatever techniques are employed, a good relationship between worker and client is essential. CT does not imply that accurate empathy, warmth and genuineness on the part of the worker can be dispensed with.

Indications and contraindications for the use of CT
The evidence suggests that CT can be an effective component in helping depressed people, especially those without psychotic symptoms. However, it may not be equally well suited to all clients. Beck (1976) has suggested that a certain amount of verbal sophistication, intelligence and a capacity for intro-spection are important client qualities in the application of CT. But, this assumption has not been tested empirically. It might well be that clients who do not tend to introspect or to rationa-lize and test out their beliefs would benefit more, or at least equally, from the therapy.

It is not clear whether CT is appropriate for people from ethnic minority and religious groups, for it seems to be a therapy that is particularly culturally bound – it was devised in America, with presumably white Americans in mind. Workers using cognitive techniques must therefore guard against an ethnocentric approach that treats any deviation from the commonly accepted norm as 'irrational'. To avoid using the therapy inappropriately, workers should follow the rule mentioned in Chapter 5 of discussing the method, its applica-tion and implications with *all* clients before using it.

Finally CT may be less useful for those people who have a perfectly clear intellectual understanding of *why* they are dis-tressed, but who continue to find it difficult to act according to their knowledge, or to curb their strong emotions. For these people, other therapeutic methods may need to be used with or instead of CT.

Summary
Cognitive therapy can be a useful method for alleviating depres-sion in many women, if it is used sensitively within a feminist perspective. The central techniques involve identifying and critically examining thoughts and beliefs which may cause distress. Women can then make more informed choices about whether to adhere to such views or to attempt to change them to less depressogenic ones. By altering perceptions and beliefs, such as those related to sex-role stereotyping, women may be enabled to live more satisfying life-styles.

Workers using CT can employ a variety of techniques to assist clients; they may suggest that women make a daily record of dysfunctional thoughts, replace negative self-statements with positive ones and/or test out their assumptions in real life situations. By these means women can accrue skills to help them cope with their depression and possibly prevent it re-occurring in the future.

Further reading

Beck, A.T. (1976) *Cognitive Therapy and the Emotional Disorders*, New York: International University Press.

Beck, A.T. and Greenberg, R.L. (1974) 'Cognitive Therapy with Depressed Women,' in V. Franks and V. Burtle (eds), *Women in Therapy*, New York: Brunner/Mazel.

Beck, A.T., Rush, A.J., Shaw, B.F. and Emery, G. (1979) *Cognitive Therapy of Depression*, New York: Guildford Press.

Williams, J.M.G. (1984) *The Psychological Treatment of Depression. A Guide to the Theory and Practice of Cognitive Behaviour Therapy*, London and Canberra: Croom Helm.

7 Working with Women in Groups

The following chapter begins with a discussion of the potential contribution that group work in general can make to helping depressed women. We then focus in more detail on assertiveness training as one particular method that can be usefully carried out in the context of groups.

Social work groups for depressed women
Group work can be an excellent method for meeting the needs of depressed women, either as the primary therapeutic approach or as a complement to other methods. Since groups provide a means by which one or two workers can reach a number of women at the same time, this method should appeal to busy SSDs. Groups are suitable for those women who do not feel too threatened to expose their feelings to others, and may be particularly useful for women who cannot or do not wish to engage in a one to one relationship with a worker.

Social workers wishing to run groups need to inform themselves about the relevant theory. They need to be aware too of the various difficulties and issues associated with setting up and leading groups. These points are discussed thoroughly by Brown (1979). It would also be useful for social workers to know some games, techniques and therapies that can be used to facilitate the group process. Ernst and Goodison's book *In Our Own Hands* (1981) is full of ideas that can be used for running groups with a feminist orientation. *The Gamester's Handbook* (Brandes and Phillips 1979) and *The Red Book of Groups* (Houston 1984) may also be helpful. Our purpose here is to review in general terms the value of groupwork for depressed women. The discussion is not intended to provide a blueprint for running a group, since the specific issues raised and methods employed in a group would be determined by its particular composition, and the needs of its members.

The value of single-sex groups for depressed women
The common causes and shared experiences of depression in

women make single-sex groups a particularly facilitative environment for growth and change. As we shall see, groups for women only, allow issues to be discussed in a way that would probably not be possible in mixed groups. A single-sex group is in many ways less risky for women and enables trust between members to be built up more quickly. It tends to create a safer environment in which women feel free to express their anger, fears and tears, thus encouraging a deeper exploration of personal and political dilemmas. Furthermore, single-sex groups prevent women from deferring to men, looking to them for approval, or allowing men to take the lead in discussions, as women often tend to do in mixed groups.

We shall now examine some of the reasons why women–only groups run from a feminist perspective can be an effective and valuable means of meeting the needs of depressed women. We shall also indicate a few of the techniques that may be employed for meeting these needs.

1. Groups can dilute the power of the worker(s), enabling power to be spread more evenly among members. Group leaders can ensure that members assume responsibility for their own growth by encouraging each woman to take time for herself within the group.
2. Groups allow women to share their ideas about ways of overcoming depression and gaining pleasure for themselves. This might be facilitated by brainstorming techniques.
3. Women meeting in groups realize that they are not alone in experiencing depression and related problems. Group leaders can encourage women to share their thoughts and feelings about being depressed and can draw out the commonality of their experiences so that they can identify with each other, thus creating a sense of unity. This may be achieved by, for example, discussing specific issues such as why women get depressed and why they get depressed more often than men. The realisation that their problems are not unique should help to reduce women's feelings of isolation and stigmatization and bring a sense of relief. Women may thus discover that they are 'normal', not 'sick' or 'mad'.
4. Groups facilitate the process of consciousness-raising and the examination of the relationship between external and

internal processes. As women share and confront their problems, they discover together which are the result of socio-political factors and which are more the consequences of personal or inter-personal difficulties. They can then make more rational decisions about what can be individually controlled and what requires action of a more political nature. Group leaders can facilitate consciousness-raising by a number of different techniques. For example, to help women to get in touch with themselves and the forces that shape them they could suggest women write their 'her-stories' and then share them with the group. Her-stories are personal accounts of growing up female in a sexist society and might include details about family life, personal relationships, schooling and employment. To generate awareness about sex-role stereotyping and society's expectations of women, group members could write out lists entitled 'Women should ...', 'Men should ...'. Women may realize from doing this the impossibility of meeting all of the inconsistent demands placed upon them. They might also see from this exercise the importance of developing expectations that are based more on their own needs and wants.

5. The group process can foster meaningful changes on an individual level. Through giving other group members permission to meet their own needs and allowing them to express their wishes and emotions, each woman can discover that she herself can claim rights which she had previously allowed others, but not herself, to exercise. Being present whilst others are working through difficulties can help each woman get closer to solving her own problems. Support and encouragement from peers enables women to alter their attitudes, behaviour and situations. Leaders can facilitate personal change by drawing on a variety of therapeutic methods, from gestalt, transactional analysis and encounter, to psychodrama, guided fantasy and body-work (see Ernst & Goodison 1981).

6. Groups facilitate catharsis. A cohesive and supportive group can enable women to release powerful emotions, either positive or negative, and move towards exploring the more 'irrational' parts of themselves. Internal obstacles to recovery and growth may be removed and overcome. Individual and collective anger, for example against

women's oppression, may be vented and then channelled into positive actions. Gestalt, encounter and body-work techniques are particularly useful in encouraging the direct expression of feelings.

7. Groups inspire and generate hope. Women who can be seen to have overcome problems inspire hope and faith in others who have not yet done so, encouraging them also to attempt changes. This is particularly valuable for depressed people who tend to feel hopeless. The opportunity to offer hope, help and support to others is also very therapeutic for depressed women, who typically view themselves as inadequate, worthless, helpless and unhelpful. Workers can also encourage a more hopeful perspective and raise self-esteem by drawing attention to women's positive achievements and strengths.

8. The group process facilitates learning of social-interaction skills. Women can model themselves on group leaders or other members and experiment with different behaviours, adopting those most appropriate and expedient for them. Workers might encourage women to role-play situations and to give feedback and positive reinforcement to the efforts of other members.

9. Groups provide an opportunity for women to learn to trust and relate closely to other women. Friendships and support networks can develop naturally from the group situation, breaking down loneliness, isolation and perhaps dependency on one man. Workers can encourage members to nurture each other and to accept the support and nurturance offered by others.

10. Groups are a pool of hidden skills and resources. Workers can encourage women to discover, value and share their skills within the group and outside it. This should help to overcome feelings of inadequacy and helplessness, raise self-esteem and encourage women to respect and value each other. Group leaders can also suggest ways and means of women learning skills that they lack, but would like to own. For example, workers might suggest members join a women's wood-workshop, or an employment or training programme.

11. Led groups can develop into self-help groups. Women can thus have an ongoing forum for learning, sharing, gaining and giving support. Workers can foster this by helping

women to develop their own leadership skills from the outset and by urging them to assume increasing responsibility for the group. Members could, for instance, identify and bring up issues for discussion, or set tasks for each other, to be carried out individually or together, in the group or outside it.

12. Groups can form the basis and impetus for women to take collective action to achieve change in the external world. Workers can help women to develop the skills and confidence to take an active part in shaping their own environment. This might be achieved through social-skills and assertiveness training, plus suggesting ideas about particular ways of campaigning, such as establishing pressure groups.

The efficacy of group work for depressed women has been noted in a number of reports (Bowman and Ware 1978; Fyfe and Howard 1982; Nelson and Wigglesworth 1983). One successful group in America had an explicitly feminist orientation (Haussmann and Halseth 1983). Although this method is not usually used with depressed adolescent or elderly women, there is no reason to presume that it would not be appropriate and effective for such clients. A feminist perspective should serve to enhance the value and efficacy of all women's groups. For, apart from factors already mentioned, it is a dynamic force which can give a group shape and cohesion, a sense of energy, purpose and direction — qualities which often seem to be lacking in groups.

We turn now to look at one particular means of helping depressed women within a group context.

Assertiveness training

Assertiveness training (AT) can be fruitfully incorporated into feminist-oriented groups, either as a single component or as the major therapeutic approach. Although techniques from AT can be used to good effect in individual therapy it appears to be particularly beneficial for trainees to learn in groups and especially single-sex groups (Brumage and Willis 1974). AT can be helpful in curbing feelings of helplessness, passivity and depression and in improving inter-personal communication (Sanchez *et al* 1980; Richey 1981). It should prove to be especially valuable to depressed women, who tend to experience greater difficulties in their inter-personal relationships and who are usually more submissive and passive than those who are not depressed (Weissman and Paykel 1974).

Before we discuss the techniques of AT we shall begin by defining what we mean by assertiveness and how it is distinguished from aggressiveness. For whilst the two are quite different, they are often confused.

Assertiveness connotes non-verbal and verbal behaviour that enables people to act in their best interests, to stand up for themselves, and to express opinions, feelings, beliefs and attitudes in a direct, honest and appropriate manner without undue anxiety (Alberti and Emmons 1982). Assertive people exercise rights without denying or violating the rights and feelings of others, for assertiveness conveys respect for oneself and respect, although not necessarily deference, to other people. The consequences of assertive behaviour should be positive to the individual, since pleasant opportunities are exploited and unpleasant ones avoided or defused. The effects of increased assertiveness should also be of benefit to others, since mutual respect is encouraged and resentment resulting from unarticulated desires diminished. Clear, honest communication should become the accepted norm.

Examples of assertive behaviour include taking initiatives, refusing requests, requesting behaviour changes, complimenting others, disagreeing with others and effectively handling criticism. However, such behaviours, as Alberti and Emmons (1982) note, are 'person- and situation-specific, not universal.' Although they may be appropriate for most people and circumstances, individual differences based, for example, on cultural or ethnic background 'may create an entirely different set of personal circumstances which would change the nature of "appropriateness" in assertive behaviour' (Alberti and Emmons 1982, p.17).

In contrast to assertiveness, aggressive behaviour includes hostile words or actions which coerce, dominate, humiliate or put others down. The recipients of such messages usually feel hurt, defensive, humiliated, frustrated and angry.

Women have usually been socialized to be passive and non-assertive. They are often rewarded for such modes of behaviour and discouraged not only from aggressive, but also from assertive, actions. As we have seen, however, the traditional feminine role which emphasizes non-assertiveness and passivity has made women vulnerable to helplessness, emotional distress and depression. For, non-assertion means failing to stand up for one's rights or failing to honestly express one's thoughts, feelings and beliefs, thus allowing them to be disregarded or violated by others. Feelings of self-hatred plus resentment towards other people are common in women who are depressed and non-assertive. Through AT, however, women can learn more effective and open ways of communicating and can gain control over situations. By developing a more androgynous identity they can become more balanced people who can exercise choice over the way they act, rather than living according to the dictates of their socialization. AT helps women to get in touch with their own needs and power, to learn that they have rights, and to be strong and effective as well as nurturant and sensitive.

Assertiveness training procedures and techniques
Jakubowski (1977), a prominent worker in this field, identifies four phases to assertion training:

1. Helping clients to distinguish between assertive, aggressive, and non-assertive behaviour; motivating clients to become more assertive, and increasing clients' awareness of their own behaviour;
2. Helping clients to identify and accept their inter-personal rights and to develop a belief system which will support their assertive behaviour;
3. Reducing or removing psychological obstacles which prevent clients from acquiring or using their assertive skills; and
4. Developing assertive skills through active practice methods.

The relative importance of these four components will depend on the members of a training group. It is likely, however, that with depressed clients each stage will need to be worked through carefully, although the phases are bound to overlap. A commitment to at least ten weekly sessions is likely to be necessary when AT is the primary therapeutic approach.

Phase 1: Understanding assertiveness, developing motivation, observing behaviour and setting goals
A primary component of AT involves helping trainees to distin-

guish between assertiveness, non-assertiveness and aggression, and allaying fears that the outcome of training will be increased aggression. The worker might like to present a range of examples of these three modes of behaviour and encourage clients to distinguish between them themselves. (Some examples are given in Alberti and Emmons 1982, pp.31–38, 80–86). Discussion may then focus on the negative consequences of non-assertive or aggressive behaviour, to help develop motivation to change.

In order to change, group members first need to become aware of their non-assertive behaviour. The examples of the different types of behaviours may begin to generate such an awareness, as may an assertiveness inventory. This is a questionnaire where respondents have to say how they would act in given situations. (An example of an assertiveness inventory can be found in Alberti and Emmons 1982, pp.40–1). Clients can also be helped to increase their awareness of non-assertive actions by the comments of workers and other group members and by the use of videos.

As a homework assignment women might be encouraged to observe their behaviour and keep an assertiveness log. This is a daily record in which trainees note both situations where they have succeeded in acting assertively and those in which they were unsuccessful in their assertive efforts. They can record here too the reasons that they believe explain their non-assertive behaviour. By this means women can learn what may be preventing them from acting assertively and when, where and with whom they have most difficulty in being assertive. Women may then be able to select specific target areas in which they want to become more assertive. Workers can help group members to prioritise targets and to set realistic goals for change, encouraging them to begin with small, low-risk steps, where the chances of success and positive reinforcements are maximised. Women can then take progressive steps up their assertiveness ladder. (For an example of such a ladder or hierarchy see Butler 1981, p.53–5).

The techniques discussed above obviously require some degree of literacy. Workers need to be sensitive to the possibility that not all women will be comfortable with writing or reading, and that therefore, other methods and tools may need to be used.

Phase 2: Identifying and accepting inter-personal rights
Many writers have formulated suitable lists of inter-personal
rights (see Figure 7.1). Group discussion can be used as a basis
for elucidating what trainees feel their rights are, and should be,
and for developing a commitment to an agreed set of rights.
Whilst many of the rights listed in Figure 7.1 might seem
simple and obvious, it may take many women, particularly
those who are exceedingly self-denigrating, a long time to inter-
nalize them.

In order to accept their inter-personal rights and develop an
assertive philosophy, women may need to question their socialization messages (signals concerning appropriate roles and
behaviours). Some cognitive therapy techniques (see Chapter 5)
may well be useful here, although the group process may itself
help members in this respect. Usually group members begin to
see that they can claim for themselves rights which formerly
they had believed only others could exercise. Also those
members who feel assured about their own rights may provide a
powerful motivation to others.

Some women may realize intellectually that they are entitled
to claim certain rights, but feel unable to accept them emotion-

1. The right to be treated with respect.
2. The right to have and express your own feelings and
   opinions.
3. The right to make mistakes.
4. The right to state your own needs and set your own
   priorities as a person independent of any roles you may
   assume.
5. The right to say no without feeling guilty.
6. The right to ask for what you want.
7. The right to have your needs regarded as equally important
   as the needs of others.
8. The right to change your mind.
9. The right to say you don't understand.
10. The right to decline responsibility for other people's
    problems.
11. The right to choose not to assert youself.

Figure 7.1 Bill of rights

Drawn and adapted from: Jakubowski (1977) and Dickson (1982).

ally or to act upon them. For these women, therapeutic techniques that are more emotionally involving, such as those derived from gestalt, may be helpful (see Ernst and Goodison 1981 for examples).

Phase 3: Removing psychological obstacles to assertion
Major obstacles to assertive behaviour are likely to be thoughts, attitudes and beliefs, particularly those associated with sex-role socialization. Negative self-statements connected with their self-image as females may continually hinder women from acting assertively. As Butler (1981) comments, 'selfish, bitchy, aggressive, unfeminine — these are the terms women have listed again and again as interfering with their self-assertion' (p.60). Group members may need to be given frequent permission to act assertively and helped to assess the appropriateness of their actions. The connections between women's lack of assertion, their depression and their socialization need to be drawn out. By this means women should not feel unnecessarily inadequate about their passive behaviour, their difficulties in acquiring assertive skills, or guilty when they are assertive. Cognitive techniques such as thought-stopping (saying stop when an unpleasant thought occurs) or replacing positive statements for negative ones, can be valuable in overcoming negative self-talk and assumptions. Butler (1981, p.74) has compiled a useful list of positive self-statements that women can use when preparing for self-assertion, when handling an assertive encounter, and when assessing the assertive experience. These techniques can be practised as part of homework assignments.

In addition to socialization messages and negative self-talk, other blocks to assertive behaviour include anxiety, nervousness and embarrassment, plus fears of criticism, rejection, anger, aggression and hurting the feelings of others. Relaxation exercises (see Lazarus 1971 and Bernstein and Borkovec 1974 for examples) may be useful to help reduce generalized anxiety whilst discussion, role play and reality-testing might help to overcome fears and other difficulties with acting assertively. It is important to remember that women should always begin to practise their assertion in those areas that create least anxiety, and where success is most likely, gradually working up to those that are most difficult. With each success, a woman's anxiety should decrease and acts of assertion should become easier to perform.

Phase 4: Developing assertive skills

A lack of assertive skills is obviously a major obstacle to self-assertion. Depressed women may need help to know exactly what is involved in direct, honest and spontaneous communication and will need a great deal of practice in developing such behaviour. They may need to practice *what* to say in certain situations as well as *how* to say it. For messages to be absolutely clear, non-verbal and verbal cues must be congruent. The components of assertive behaviour include the appropriate use of such details as eye contact, body posture, physical distance from others, facial expressions and voice tone, inflection and volume. However, there are no specific formulas or scripts for assertive expression. These will depend upon the situation and who is involved. Women will thus need to learn to judge what is appropriate when, and to work out their own style of assertive behaviour. This can be achieved partly in the AT group and partly by practice outside it.

The core techniques used to improve skills in assertion are behavioural rehearsal, modelling, coaching, prompting, feedback and reinforcement, plus homework assignments. Behavioural rehearsal involves one or more members role-playing a social interaction related to a problematic situation. The situation may be preplanned or spontaneous, roles may be varied and role-plays may be repeated several times to improve performance. Role-play may be followed by video and/or verbal feedback and instructional coaching to help members focus on the specific verbal and non-verbal components of the behaviour that convey the desired message. Initial emphasis after role-plays should be on positive feedback, then specific behaviours which may detract from the message may be discussed and suggestions for improving performances given. All group members should be encouraged to participate either in the role-play itself or in the feedback afterwards. Behavioural rehearsal allows members to learn and practise assertive skills in what should be a safe, non-threatening environment.

Modelling is another central feature of AT. The worker serves as a model during regular interaction with members as well as in selected role-plays. Group members may also serve as useful models to each other.

Homework usually involves putting into practice skills learned in the sessions. Initially, specific situations that are role-played in the training may be transferred to actual situations.

Gradually, the skills should be generalized to cover a variety of situations and types of behaviours.

During the later stages of an AT course sessions may evolve spontaneously. Group members may focus on whatever problems they are experiencing at the time, or draw on difficulties that they may have identified through an assertiveness inventory. Alternatively, sessions may revolve around specific themes. Themes or difficulties that it might be helpful for depressed women to concentrate on include: starting and developing a conversation; setting limits and learning how to say no; asking clearly for what you want; taking care of yourself and your body; acting without approval from others; living alone and combating isolation; and dealing with doctors and other professionals.

Assertive behaviour may bring unfortunate repercussions even when it is appropriate. A depressed woman attempting to become more assertive in her family may upset the balance of the system and create strains in the family relationships. She may encounter resistance to her efforts to change and other family members may refuse to cooperate, obstructing her attempts to be assertive. Recipients of assertive actions can also be hostile or aggressive in direct or indirect ways. AT must therefore emphasise the risks as well as the benefits to assertion and women should be encouraged to think about the implications that changes in themselves may create in their families. They need to be given permission to discuss any fears they may have as well as the difficulties or obstacles they may face when attempting to be assertive. Trainees should learn how to assess situations and judge when assertive behaviour will be beneficial and/or may be met with criticism, hostility or resistance. They should then be taught assertive skills for dealing with hostile or negative responses from others (see Butler 1981; Alberti and Emmons 1982).

In feminist oriented AT groups (as in other feminist therapeutic groups) workers should be sure that the trainees fully comprehend the training process, so that they may not only take an active part in current training sessions but would also be encouraged to develop tools for self-help in the future.

Example of an AT group
Two feminist psychiatric social workers ran a ten week AT group in the community for twelve mildly depressed, isolated

and/or anxious women. The group primarily aimed to help the women to combat their lack of confidence and their feelings of loneliness and helplessness, through the learning of some basic assertiveness skills.

The first few sessions of the group focused on the meaning of assertiveness, both in general terms and to each individual woman. Some time needed to be spent on discussing the distinctions between assertiveness and aggressiveness and on allaying women's fears of becoming aggressive. Many group members had a double standard of assertiveness for men and women, that is, what was seen as assertive behaviour for men was labelled as aggressive for women. The workers tried to draw out the social reasons for this.

The early sessions also aimed to help the women to generate an awareness of their own particular 'assertive style' and how they wanted to change. Women quickly came to recognize behaviour patterns in themselves and were also relieved to find that others had similar difficulties. However, many found it hard to be specific about what they wanted to change, and the workers felt, in retrospect, that insufficient time was spent helping women individually with their 'assertiveness ladders'.

After the first few sessions, meetings began with feedback from homework and group members relating their successes as well as their difficulties with assertion. Sessions then continued by focusing on specific themes, such as inter-personal rights, dealing with anger and conflict, obstacles to assertion and body language. The workers drew on a range of methods to facilitate learning and sharing. At different times there were group discussions, exercises in pairs, small group role-plays, workers role-playing and modelling specific techniques, written tasks done individually and so on. This variety made sessions more interesting, and was also intended to ensure that each woman had the chance of learning and participating in ways she felt comfortable with. The more shy and anxious women found it difficult to participate in group discussions and some were initially resistant to role-playing.

A persistent obstacle faced by the women was their low self-image and consequent fear that others would think ill of them if they acted assertively. The workers ongoing task was thus to boost the women's self-esteem through the general group process, as well as through specific confidence building exercises. Another major theme running throughout the course was the difficulty of being assertive with close family members. Although some successes were gained in this area, many women continued to find it easier to be assertive in less intimate relationships.

By the end of ten weeks the group had become cohesive and the members had gained considerable support and encouragement from each other. Through the group many had realized for the first time that they could *choose* how to act and that their behaviour was largely within their control. Strides had been made in breaking down the women's sense of isolation and many felt more confident and better about themselves. The members requested more sessions and it was agreed to have a follow-up after a few months. In the meantime some women continued meeting together for ongoing learning and support.

This is what some women have said about AT:

> The course makes you think about assertiveness. Now when I'm going to say or do something I think first, how can I do this assertively, rather than jumping straight in or screaming and shouting?

> I haven't felt so depressed since the course because I know how to handle things better. I don't let things get me down so much, I just cope with them better.

> Before the group I used to just sit back and let things carry on and I wouldn't complain, but now I don't, now I say what I want. I push for things instead of just giving up and I won't let people walk over me so much, I don't let myself be bullied ... I've got the courage to do things I never would have done before, like with the solicitor and my ex-husband. Now I feel it's my right to get maintenance so I've taken my husband back to court ...

> It's helped me a lot with the children. Now if I threaten them I don't back down, whereas before I always used to.

> The group helps you to take your courage in your hands ... It made me think about doing things like standing up for my rights at work, when before I just wouldn't have bothered.

I think the group helped to boost my confidence and gave me more courage to say what I think.

I'm more honest about things now, instead of making excuses or getting into rows.

The value of AT

The positive effects of AT have been reported in a number of studies (Wolfe and Fodor 1977; Sanchez *et al* 1980; Richey 1981). Trainees seem to benefit in a number of ways, including improving their inter-personal skills, challenging their socialization messages and developing a belief system which fully acknowledges their personal rights. Also, female trainees in assertiveness classes seem to gain a sense of relief when they realise that their more passive stance is not merely a reflection of individual inadequacy, but is engendered by society's expectation of women's behaviour (Gottlieb *et al* 1983).

Although rarely utilised at present, AT may well be helpful in general social work practice, as well as for the client group we are concerned with here. It would seem particularly useful for social work clients, since in addition to helping with their inter-personal relations, it fosters the skills necessary to attain resources and services in the community with minimal assistance from the caring professions.

Summary

In this chapter we have looked at the value of groupwork in general, as well as at one particular approach (assertiveness training) that can be of benefit to depressed women. Groups give women the opportunity to share and develop a unity with each other, to examine their feelings and behaviour and to develop new modes of acting and reacting. Groups also enable women to initiate collective as well as individual change. Through AT women learn to stand up for their rights whilst not denying the rights of others. They discover how to communicate more effectively, honestly and directly. AT can help depressed women to overcome feelings of helplessness and passivity and it encourages them to take charge of their lives. Working with women in groups is a productive and effective means by which social workers can help women not only to overcome their immediate problems, but also to help themselves in the future.

Further reading

On groups:

Brandes, D. and Phillips, H. (1977) *The Gamesters' Handbook*, London: Hutchinson.

Brown, A. (1979) *Groupwork*, London: Heinemann/Gower.

Ernst, S. and Goodison, L. (1981) *In Our Own Hands*, London: The Women's Press.

Fyfe, E. and Howard, A. (1982) 'Working It Out Together,' *Community Care*, 432, 19–20.

Gottlieb, N., Burden, D., McCormick, R. and Nicarthy, G. (1983) 'The Distinctive Attributes of Feminist Groups,' *Social Work with Groups*, 3/4, 81–93.

Haussmann, M.J. and Halseth, J.H. (1983) 'Re-examining Women's Roles: A Feminist Group Approach to Decreasing Depression in Women,' *Social Work With Groups*, 6, 3/4, 105–15.

Houston, G. (1984) *The Red Book of Groups*, London: The Rochester Foundation.

Nelson, B. and Wigglesworth, S. (1983) 'Setting up a Group for Depressed and Isolated Women,' *Community Care*, 26 May, 17.

Remocker, A.J. and Storch, E.T. (1979) *Action Speaks Louder. A Handbook of Nonverbal Group Techniques*, London: Churchill Livingstone.

Yalom, I. (1975) *The Theory and Practice of Group Psychotherapy*, New York: Basic Books.

On assertiveness training:

Alberti, R.E. and Emmons, M.L. (1982) *Your Perfect Right: A Guide to Assertive Behaviour*, California: Impact, 4th edn.

Butler, P.E. (1981) *Self-Assertion for Women*, New York: Harper and Row.

Dickson, A. (1982) *A Woman in Your Own Right*, London: Quartet Books.

Dickson, A. (1985) *The Mirror Within*, London: Quartet Books.

Galinsky, M.J., Schopler, J.H., Safier, E.J. and Gambrill, E.D. (1978) 'Assertion Training for Public Welfare Clients,' *Social Work with Groups*, 1, 4, 365–79.

Jakubowski, P.A. (1977a) 'Assertive Behavior and Clinical Problems of Women,' and (1977b) 'Self-Assertion Training

Procedures for Women,' in E.I. Rawlings and D.K. Carter (eds) *Psychotherapy for Women*, Illinois: Thomas Publisher.

Phelps, S. and Austin, N. (1975) *The Assertive Woman*, California: Impact Publishers.

8 Conclusion: Looking Forward

In this book we have seen that social workers can play a major role in helping women to overcome depression. However, at present they are often constrained by the structure of their own organisations and sometimes limited by inadequate training. Clearly, the social work contribution to women with depression would be greatly enhanced if appropriate changes were made in these areas. CQSW courses should place more emphasis upon the needs and interests of women and all people with mental health problems, and should encourage the development of therapeutic as well as practical skills in their students. Similarly, SSDs should take much greater account of the needs of women, both as workers and clients, and give higher priority to people suffering mental or emotional distress in the provision of social work support and material resources. Acceptance and encouragement of a feminist oriented practice would not go amiss either. Feminist social workers, as we have already suggested, could play a part in instigating such changes.

Improvements in social work training and practice are of course not in themselves sufficient to ensure that the emotional distress of women is adequately attended to. For, unfortunately, depressed women are often ill-served by the National Health Service as well as by the social services. Thus the mental health system as a whole must be the target for change.

The imminent closure of most long-stay psychiatric hospitals and the policy of community care means that the shape of the mental health services in Britain is already beginning to change. Currently, there is much discussion and debate on a national as well as a local level about the future provision of services for the 'mentally ill'. Social workers can make a valuable contribution to this debate. Indeed, since SSDs are likely to take an increasingly prominent role in providing such services, it is imperative that social workers have a say in the formulation of policies and practices. The creation of a new mental health service must, however, also rest substantially upon the collective wisdom and views of those who have experienced the existing system as consumers.

Feminist workers could join with users and ex-users of the mental health system and their relatives to provide a strong and collective voice with which to influence the direction of policy and provision in the mental health field. By this means they could try to campaign for a mental health service that is genuinely responsive to the requirements of women and committed to combatting the unnecessary distress and depression in our society. After discussions with depressed women, ex-mental health patients and feminist workers about what such a service might be like, a number of features have emerged as being central and essential. Primarily, it would have to take as its starting point the needs and interests of consumers, as expressed by them, regardless of sex, age, race, class, disability and so on. This means having a wide range of free, local and *accessible* services, ensuring continuity of care and offering individuals choice and the opportunity for self-determination. Resources would need to be staffed by workers who, whatever their training, are concerned with enabling women to act on their own behalf and who are committed to a non-sexist, non-oppressive approach. As part of this approach, women would be allowed and encouraged to express their pain and distress (non-violently) without fear of being labelled 'mad' and without immediately incurring the risk of being drugged or contained. At the same time, there would have to be a full acknowledgement that such human distress is frequently the result of social inequalities and oppression and not merely a symptom of 'personal inadequacy'.

The actual realization of such a service requires, at the very least, the commitment and cooperation of all the relevant statutory and voluntary bodies, a sufficient number of enthusiastic and suitably trained workers and of course, the necessary financial support from central government, without which little can be achieved. Additionally, the creation of a consumer-centred mental health service necessarily demands a profound change in attitudes as well as practices, and a fundamental reappraisal of the traditional professional response. In sum, we need a different style of service — a change in form as well as content.

The resources set up by the women's movement, such as women's refuges, women's therapy and counselling centres and hostels for women who have left psychiatric hospitals, provide positive examples of the type of services that are needed in

Appendix: Some Useful Addresses

Voluntary and self-help organisations

The following is a list of some national organisations that have local groups or contacts around the country. Many give information and advice to professionals as well as to individuals seeking help.

Fellowship of Depressives Anonymous
National Office
36 Chestnut Avenue
Beverley
N. Humberside HU17 9QU

Support groups, newsletter, pen friend scheme. Sae for information.

Portia Trust
15 Senhouse Street
Maryport
Cumbria CA15 6AB
090-081-2114

Network of volunteers offering help and support to those who get into trouble with the law through depression and stress.

Tranx
17 Peel Road
Wealdstone
Middlesex HA1 2EZ
01-427-2065

Information, advice and support groups for those wanting to come off tranquillizers.

Association for Postnatal Illness
7 Gowan Avenue
London SW6
01–731–7018

Network of phone volunteers.

Meet-a-Mum Association (MAMA)
26a Cumnor Hill
Oxford OX2 9HA

Support groups for women with post-natal depression. Sae for information.

Compassionate Friends
6 Denmark Street
Bristol BS1 5DG
0272–292778

Groups for bereaved parents.

Cruse
Cruse House
126 Sheen Road
Richmond
Surrey TW9 1UR
01–940–4818/9047

Individual support for the bereaved.

Stillbirth and Neonatal Death Society
Argyle House
29–31 Euston Road
London NW1
01–833–2851

Support groups for parents who have lost a baby.

Organisation for Parents Under Stress (OPUS)
26 Manor Drive
Pickering
Yorkshire YO18 8DD

Support groups and telephone listening service. Send sae for local groups.

Mothers Apart from Their Children (MATCH)
c/o B.M. Problems
London WC1 3XX

Support groups for women living apart from their children.

National Association of Carers
c/o Medway Homes
Balfour Road
Rochester
Kent ME4 6QU
0634-813981

Information, advice and support groups for carers.

Women's organisations and groups

Women and mental health groups

Bristol Women and Mental Health Network
c/o The Women's Centre
44 The Grove
Bristol 1
0272-522248

Members composed of consumers, relatives, workers and lay people interested in campaigning for change in the mental health system. The network also acts as an umbrella organisation for local women and mental health groups including a 'survivors' group and a group looking into setting up a crisis service for women.

DAWN (Drugs, Alcohol and Women — Nationally)
140 Queen Victoria Street
London EC4U 4BX
01-236-8125

A pressure group working for better understanding and treatment of drug (prescribed and non-prescribed) and alcohol problems in women. Local groups around the country.

London Women and Mental Health
c/o WHIC
52–54 Featherstone Street
London EC1 8RT
01–251–6580

Women in Need of Gaining Strength (WINGS)
c/o The Women's Centre
61a Broughton Street
Edinburgh
031–557–3179

Aims to set up alternative/complementary mental health facilities for women.

Women's Therapeutic Community Group
c/o Aggie Gatrubika/Dimpla McLellia
24 Keighley Road
Bradford 8
0274–490371

Aims to set up a therapeutic community for women in West Yorkshire.

Counselling and therapy centres

The following centres offer individual and group therapy to women either free of charge or for a fee according to income. Most centres are also involved in initiating and supporting women's self-help groups and run training workshops for women in the caring professions.

Birmingham Women's Counselling and Therapy Centre
43 Ladywood
Middleway
Birmingham 16
021–455–8677

Leeds Women's Counselling and Therapy Service
Oxford Chambers
Oxford Place
Leeds LS13 8AX
0532–455725

Oxford Women's Counselling Centre
Highcroft House
Tanners Lane
Eynsham
Oxon
0865–881268

Pellin South London Feminist Therapy Centre
Pellin Centre
43 Killyon Road
London SW8
01–622–0148

The Women's Therapy Centre
6 Manor Gardens
London N7
01–263–6200

Other services for women

Head On
c/o Link, Glasgow Association for Mental Health
2 Queens Crescent
Glasgow G4 9BW
041–332–3186

Runs support groups on different aspects of women's mental health.

Incest Survivors
c/o A Woman's Place
Hungerford House
Victoria Embankment
London WC2
01–836–6081

Information on local self-help and campaign groups.

Islington Women and Mental Health
Caxton House
129 St John's Way
London N19
01–281–2673

Telephone crisis line, drop-in service, support groups.

Rape Crisis
PO Box 69
London WC1
01-278-3956
01-837-1600   (24-hour crisis line)

The national office for information on local centres that offer
counselling and advice for women who have been sexually
assaulted.

WIRES (Women's Information, Referral and Enquiry Service)
PO Box 20
Oxford
0865-240991

A national information service that can put women in touch
with a huge variety of women's groups and centres around the
country.

Womankind
c/o The Settlement
43 Ducie Road
Barton Hill
Bristol BS5 0AX
0272-556164

Initiates and supports self-help groups on the theme of
women's mental health.

Women's Aid
374 Gray's Inn Road
London WC1
01-837-9316

The national office for information on local refuges for women
and children escaping domestic violence. Also operates a 24-
hour help line.

The Women's Alcohol Centre
254 St Pauls Road
London N1
01-226-4581

A residential and non-residential service offering individual and
group counselling to women with drink problems.

Women's Health Information Centre
52–54 Featherstone Street
London EC1Y 8ET
01–251–6580

A national information and resource centre on all aspects of women's health, including mental health. Can put women in touch with local groups around the country.

Campaigning Organisations

The British Network for Alternatives to Psychiatry
c/o 158 Rivermead Court
Hurlingham
London SW6

Part of an international network aiming to promote alternatives to the current psychiatric system. Members are composed of consumers of psychiatric services, workers in the mental health field and interested lay people.

Campaign Against Psychiatric Oppression (CAPO)
c/o 18 Seymour Buildings
Seymour Place
London W1H 5TQ

Consumers and allies campaigning for alternatives to the present psychiatric system, and greater consumer participation in existing services.

MIND (National Association for Mental Health)
22 Harley Street
London W1N 2ED
01–637–0741

Aims to promote better mental health services and to further the interests of people with mental health problems and their families. There are approximately 150 local associations offering a casework and advisory service with wide-ranging information on local mental health facilities. MIND also produces publications and runs workshops and training days for workers in the field. In addition there is a policy working party called

'Women in Mind' composed of workers from national MIND and other interested groups, to consider the needs and promote the interests of women with mental health problems. They also have information on mental health facilities for women around the country. Contact Laureen Levy or Alison Cobb at the above address.

Survivors Speak Out
c/o Contact
Tontine Road Centre
Tontine Road
Chesterfield
Derbyshire
0246-74898

A national contact for local 'survivors'/consumer groups. Aims to empower the consumers of the mental health system and campaign for radical alternatives to it.

Professional bodies

British Association of Social Workers
Mental Health Special Interest Group
c/o Bob Fitzpatrick
Park Lane Special Hospital
Maghull
Liverpool
051-520-2244

Group for the Advancement of Psychodynamics and Psychotherapy in Social Work (GAPS)
c/o Mrs E Smith
45 Heath View
East Finchley
London N2
01-883-9926

Meetings, conferences, study days, newsletter and publications, supervision scheme.

Interdisciplinary Association of Mental Health Workers
University of Surrey
Department of Educational Studies
Guildford
Surrey 6UZ 5XH
0483-571281

Aims to improve cooperation in mental health services for the benefit of those who use them. Offers conferences, training courses, local groups and publications etc.

References

Abraham, K. (1911) 'Notes on the Psychoanalytic Investigation and Treatment of Manic-depressive Insanity and Allied Conditions,' in *Selected Papers on Psychoanalysis*, London: Hogarth Press, 1949, 137–56.

Abramson, L.Y., Seligman, M.E.P., and Teasdale, J.D. (1978) 'Learned Helplessness in Humans: Critique and Reformulation,' *Journal of Abnormal Psychology*, 87, 1, 49–75.

Ahmed, S. (1978) 'Asian Girls and Culture Conflicts,' *Social Work Today*, 9, 47, 14–16.

Ahmed, S. (1983) 'Blinkered by Background,' *Community Care*, 13 October, 20–22.

Alberti, R.E. and Emmons, M.L. (1982) *Your Perfect Right: A Guide to Assertive Behaviour*, California: Impact, 4th edition.

Ali Khan, A. (1983) 'The Mental Health of the Asian Community in an East London Health District, in A. Burke, N. Malik and A. Ali Khan (eds) *Care in the Community: Keeping It Local*, a report of MIND's Annual Conference, London: MIND.

Arieti, S. and Bemporad, J. (1978) *Severe and Mild Depression*, London: Tavistock Publications.

Aslin, A.L. (1977) 'Feminist and Community Mental Health Center Psychotherapists' Expectations of Mental Health for Women,' *Sex Roles*, 3, 6, 537–44.

Bart, P.B. (1971) 'Depression in Middle-Aged Women,' in V. Gornick and B.K. Moran (eds) *Woman in Sexist Society*, New York: Basic Books.

Beck, A.T. (1976) *Cognitive Therapy and the Emotional Disorders*, New York: International University Press.

Beck, A.T. and Greenberg, R.L. (1974) 'Cognitive Therapy with Depressed Women,' in V. Franks and V. Burtle (eds) *Women in Therapy*, New York: Brunner/Mazel.

Beck, A.T., Rush, A.J., Shaw, B.F. and Emery, G. (1979) *Cognitive Therapy of Depression*, New York: The Guildford Press.

Belle, D. (ed.) (1982) *Lives in Stress*, New York: Sage.

Belotti, E.G. (1975) *Little Girls*, London: Writers and Readers Publishing Co-operative.

Bem, S. (1974) 'The Measurement of Psychological Androgyny,' *Journal of Consulting and Clinical Psychology*, 42, 155–62.

Bem, S. (1975) 'Sex-role Adaptability: One Consequence of Psychological Androgyny,' *Journal of Personality and Social Psychology*, 31, 634–43.

Berlin, S. (1976) 'Better Work With Women Clients,' *Social Work*, 21, 6, 492–7.

Bernard, J. (1976) 'Homosociality and Female Depression,' *Journal of Social Issues*, 32, 4, 213–38.

Bernstein, D.A. and Borkovec, T.D. (1974) *Progressive Relaxation Training*, Champaign: Research Press.

Bibring, E. (1953) 'The Mechanism of Depression,' in P. Greenacre (ed.) *Affective Disorders*, New York: I.U.P.

The Birmingham Women and Social Work Group (1985) 'Women and Social Work in Birmingham,' in E. Brook and A. Davis (eds) *Women, The Family and Social Work*, London and New York:Tavistock Publications.

Bowlby, J. (1969, 1980) *Attachment and Loss*, Vols. 1 and 3, Harmondsworth: Penguin Books.

Bowman, K. and Ware, P. (1978) 'Group Therapy with Middle Aged Depressives,' *Social Work Today*, 10, 1, 19–20.

Brandes, D. and Phillips, H. (1977) *The Gamesters' Handbook*, London: Hutchinson.

Broverman, I., Broverman, D., Clarkson, F., Rosenkrantz, P. and Vogal, S. (1970) 'Sex-role Stereotypes and Clinical Judgements of Mental Health,' *Journal of Consulting and Clinical Psychology*, 34, 1–7.

Brown, A. (1979) *Groupwork*, London: Heinemann (now published by Gower).

Brown, G.W., Brochlain, M. and Harris, T. (1975) 'Social Class and Psychiatric Disturbance Among Women in an Urban Population,' *Sociology*, 9, 225–54.

Brown, G.W. and Harris, T. (1978) *Social Origins of Depression*, London: Tavistock Publications.

Brown, C.R. and Hellinger, M.C. (1975) 'Therapists' Attitudes Towards Women,' *Social Work*, 24, 4, 266–70.

Brumage, M.E. and Willis, M.H. (1974) 'How 3 Variables Influence the Outcome of Group Assertive Training,' Quoted in P.A. Jakubowski, (1977) 'Self-Assertion Training

Procedures for Women,' in E.I. Rawlings and D.K. Carter (eds) *Psychotherapy for Women*, Illinois: Thomas Publisher.

Burke, A.W. (1984) 'Racism and Psychological Disturbance Among West Indians in Britain,' *The International Journal of Social Psychiatry*, 30, 1 and 2, 50–68.

Burke, R.J. and Weir, T. (1978) 'Sex Differences in Adolescent Life Stress, Social Support and Wellbeing,' *Journal of Psychology*, 98, 277–88.

Burns, D.D. and Beck, A.T. (1978) 'Cognitive Behavior Modification of Mood Disorders,' in Foreyt, J.P. and Rattigen, D.P. (eds) *Cognitive Behavior Therapy Research and Application*, New York: Plenum Press.

Butler, A. and Pritchard, C. (1983) *Social Work and Mental Illness*, London: Macmillan.

Butler, P.E. (1981) *Self-Assertion for Women*, New York: Harper and Row.

Campling, J. (1981) (ed.) *Images of Ourselves: Women With Disabilities Talking*, London: Routledge and Kegan Paul.

Chester, R. (1985) The Rise of the Neo-conventional Family, *New Society*, 72, 1167, 185–8.

Clare, A. (1980) *Psychiatry in Dissent*, London: Tavistock Publications.

Cooper, B., Harwin, B.G., Depla, C. and Shepherd, M. (1975) 'Mental Health Care in the Community: an Evaluative Study,' *Psychological Medicine*, 5, 4, 372–80.

Cooperstock, R. and Lennard, H.L. (1979) 'Some Social Meanings of Tranquilizer Use,' *Sociology of Health and Illness*, 1, 3, 331–47.

Corney, R.H. and Clare, A.W. (1983) 'The Effectiveness of Attached Social Workers in the Management of Depressed Women in General Practice,' *British Journal of Social Work*, 13, 1, 57–74.

C.R.E. (Commission for Racial Equality) (1976) *Aspects of Mental Health in a Multi-Cultural Society*, London: C.R.E.

Crompton, M. (1982) *Adolescents and Social Workers*, London: Heinemann (now published by Gower).

Curran, V. and Golombok, S. (1985) *Bottling It Up*, London: Faber.

Dailey, D.M. (1980) 'Are Social Workers Sexists? A Replication,' *Social Work*, 25, 46–50.

D.H.S.S. (1978) *Social Service Teams: The Practitioners' View*, London: H.M.S.O.

Dickson, A. (1982) *A Woman in Your Own Right*, London: Quartet Books.

Dohrenwend, B.P. and Dohrenwend, B.S. (1976) 'Sex Differences and Psychiatric Disorders,' *American Journal of Sociology*, 81, 6, 1447–54.

Edmonds, J. (1982) 'Poverty and Race; Disadvantage in the Labour Market,' in R. Lister and S. Hart (eds) *Poverty*, 51, 3–7, London: CPAG.

Eichenbaum, L. and Orbach, S. (1982) *Outside In Inside Out*, Harmondsworth: Penguin.

Eichenbaum, L. and Orbach, S. (1984) *What Do Women Want*, Glasgow: Fontana.

Eichenbaum, L. and Orbach, S. (1985) *Understanding Women*, Harmondsworth: Penguin.

Elizabeth, R. (1983) 'De-privatising Depression', *Spare Rib*, 130, 18–20.

Epstein, L.J. (1976) 'Depression in the Elderly,' *Journal of Gerontology*, 31, 3, 278–82.

Erikson, E. (1963) 'The Inner and Outer Space: Reflections on Womanhood,' *Daedalus*, 93, 582–600.

Erikson, E. (1968) *Identity: Youth and Crisis*, New York: Norton.

Ernst, S. and Goodison, L. (1981) *In Our Own Hands*, London: The Women's Press.

Fabrikant, B. (1974) 'The Psychotherapist and the Female Patient: Perceptions, Misconceptions and Change,' in V. Franks and V. Burtle, (eds) *Women in Therapy*, New York: Brunner/Mazel.

Finch, J. and Groves, D. (1985) 'Old Girl, Old Boy: Gender Divisions in Social Work With the Elderly,' in E. Brook and A. Davis, (eds) *Women, The Family and Social Work*, London: Tavistock Publications.

Fisher, M., Newton, C. and Sainsbury, E. (1984) *Mental Health Social Work Observed*, London: George Allen and Unwin.

Francis, W. (1984) 'Intercultural Therapy: Out of the Text-books and into the Consulting Room, *Community Care*, 25 October, 19–20.

Freden, L. (1982) *Psychosocial Aspects of Depression*, New York: Wiley.

Freud, S. (1917) 'Mourning and Melancholia,' *Standard Edn.* Vol. 14 (1957) London: Hogarth Press. Reprinted in *On*

Metapsychology: The Theory of Psychoanalysis, (1984) Harmondsworth: Penguin.

Freud, S. (1925) 'Some Psychical Consequences of the Anatomical Distinction between the Sexes,' *Standard Edn.* Vol. 19 (1961) London: Hogarth Press. Reprinted in *On Sexuality*, (1977) Harmondsworth: Penguin.

Freud, S. (1931) 'Female Sexuality,' *Standard Edn.* Vol. 21 (1961) London: Hogarth Press. Reprinted in *On Sexuality*, (1977) Harmondsworth: Penguin.

Freud, S. (1933) 'Femininity', *Standard Edn.* Vol. 22 (1964) London: Hogarth Press. Reprinted in *New Introductory Lectures on Psychoanalysis*, (1973) Harmondsworth: Penguin

Friedman, A.S. (1975) 'Interaction of Drug Therapy with Marital Therapy in Depressive Patients,' *Archives of General Psychiatry*, 32, 619–37.

Froggatt, A. (1983) 'Jobs for the Girls?,' *Social Work Today*, 14, 43, 7–9.

Fyfe, E. and Howard, A. (1982) 'Working It Out Together,' *Community Care*, 432, 19–20.

Gottlieb, N., Burden, D., McCormick, R., and Nicarthy, G. (1983) 'The Distinctive Attributes of Feminist Groups,' *Social Work with Groups*, 3/4, 81–93.

Gove, W.R. (1972) 'The Relationship between Sex Roles, Marital Status and Mental Illness,' *Social Forces*, 51, 1, 34–44.

Gove, W.R. and Tudor, J.F. (1973) 'Adult Sex Roles and Mental Illness,' *American Journal of Sociology*, 78, 812–35.

Hare-Mustin, R. (1978) 'A Feminist Approach to Family Therapy,' *Family Process*, 17, June, 181–94.

Haussmann, M.J. and Halseth, J.H. (1983) 'Re-examining Women's Roles: A Feminist Group Approach to Decreasing Depression in Women,' *Social Work with Groups*, 6, 3/4, 105–15.

Hemmings, S. (ed.) (1985) *A Wealth of Experience. The Lives of Older Women*, London: Pandora Press.

Houston, G. (1984) *The Red Book of Groups*, London: The Rochester Foundation.

Hudson, B.L. (1982) *Social Work with Psychiatric Patients*, London: Macmillan.

Huxley, P. (1985) *Social Work Practice in Mental Health*, Aldershot: Gower.

Huxley, P. and Fitzpatrick, R. (1984) 'Probable Extent of Minor Mental Illness in Adult Clients of Social Workers: a Pilot Study,' *British Journal of Social Work*, 14, 67–73.

Jakubowski, P.A. (1977) 'Self-Assertion Training Procedures for Women,' in E.I. Rawlings and D.K. Carter (eds) *Psychotherapy for Women*, Illinois: Thomas Publisher.

Jones, C. (1983) *State Social Work and the Working Class*, London: Macmillan.

Jones, D.A. and Vetter, N.J. (1984) *A Survey of Those Who Care for the Elderly at Home: Their Problems and Their Needs*, London: Social Science and Medicine.

Jones, L., Simpson, D., Brown, A.C., Bainton, D. and McDonald, H. (1984) 'Prescribing Psychotropic Drugs in General Practice: a 3 Year Study,' *British Medical Journal*, 289, 20 October, 1045.

Joseph, A. (1985) 'Light in Dark Corners,' *Guardian*, 19 June.

Klein, M. (1935) 'A contribution to the Psychogenesis of Manic-depressive States,' in *Love, Guilt and Reparation*, New York: Delacoite Press, 1975, 262–89.

Kovacs, M., Rush, A.J., Beck, A.T. and Hollon, S.D. (1981) 'Depressed Out-patients Treated with Cognitive Therapy or Pharmacotherapy: a One-year Follow-up,' *Archives of General Psychiatry*, 38, 33–9.

Lazarus, A.A. (1968) 'Learning Theory and the Treatment of Depression,' *Behaviour Research and Therapy*, 6, 83–9.

Lazarus, A. (1971) *Behaviour Therapy and Beyond*, New York: McGraw Hill.

Lazarus, A.A. (1976) 'Multimodal Behavioral Treatment of Depression,' in A.A. Lazarus (ed.) *Multimodal and Behavior Therapy*, New York: Springer.

Letts, P. (1983) *Double Struggle: Sex Discrimination and One-parent Families*, London: National Council for One Parent Families.

Lewinsohn, P.M. (1974) 'A Behavioural Approach to Depression,' in R.J. Friedman and H.M. Katz (eds) *The Psychology of Depression: Contemporary Theory and Research*, Washington DC: Winston.

Lidz, T. (1968) *The Person*, New York: Basic Books.

Littlewood, R. and Lipsedge, M. (1982) *Aliens and Alienists*, Harmondsworth: Penguin.

Llewelyn, S. and Osborn, K. (1983) 'Women as Clients and Therapists,' in D. Pilgrim (ed.) *Psychology and Psycho-*

therapy, London: Routledge and Kegan Paul.

Maccoby, E. and Jacklin, C. (1974) *The Psychology of Sex Differences*, California: Stanford University Press.

Macdonald, B. and Rich, C. (1984) *Look Me In The Eye*, London: The Women's Press.

McNeill Taylor, L. (1983) *Living with Loss*, Glasgow: Fontana.

McQuaker, B.C. and Specht, R. (1982) 'Feminist Perspective?' (Letter), *Social Work*, 27, 2, 203–4.

Malik, N. (1983) 'Mental Health Needs in a Multi-cultural Community,' in A. Burke, N. Malik and Ali Khan (eds) *Care in the Community: Keeping it Local*, A report of MIND's Annual Conference. London: MIND.

Martin, J. and Roberts, C. (1984) *Women and Employment: a Lifetime Perspective*, London: H.M.S.O.

Mednick, M., Tangri, S.S. and Hoffman, L.W. (eds) (1975) *Women and Achievement*, New York: Wiley.

Melville, J. (1984) *The Tranquillizer Trap and How To Get Out Of It*, Glasgow: Fontana.

Moss, H.A. (1970) 'Sex, Age and State as Determinants of Mother-Infant Interaction,' in K. Danziger (ed.) *Readings in Child Socialization*, Oxford: Pergamon Press.

Moss, P. and Plewis, I. (1977) 'Mental Distress in Mothers of Pre-school Children in Inner London,' *Psychological Medicine*, 7, 641–52.

Murphy, E. (1982) 'Social Origins of Depression in Old Age,' *British Journal of Psychiatry*, 141, 135–42.

Murphy, P. (1985) 'Ageing,' in L. Steiner-Scott (ed.) *Personally Speaking*, Dublin: Attic Press.

Nairne, K. and Smith, G. (1984) *Dealing with Depression*, London: The Women's Press.

Nelson, B. and Wigglesworth, S. (1983) 'Setting up a Group for Depressed and Isolated Women,' *Community Care*, 26 May, 17.

Nowacki, C.M. and Poe, C.A. (1973) 'The Concept of Mental Health as Related to Sex of Person Perceived,' *Journal of Consulting and Clinical Psychology*, 40, 1, 160.

Numa, S. (1984) 'Some Issues Affecting Afro-Caribbean Women,' in *Issues on Women: Cultural Perspectives*, The Conference Report of the Transcultural Psychiatry Society, April, 33–39.

Oakley, A. (1974) *The Sociology of Housework*, London: Martin Robertson.

Oakley, A. (1976) *Housewife*, Harmondsworth: Penguin.

Oakley, A. (1980) *Women Confined*, Oxford: Martin Robertson.

Olsen, M.R. (ed.) (1984) *Social Work and Mental Health. A Guide for the Approved Social Worker*. London and New York: Tavistock Publications.

Parkes, M. (1972) *Bereavement*, London: Tavistock Publications.

Paykel, E.S., Myers, J.K., Dienelt, M.N., Klerman, G.L., Lindenthal, J.J. and Pepper, M. (1969) 'Life Events and Depression,' *Archives of General Psychiatry*, 21, December.

Pearlin, L.I. and Johnson, J.S. (1977) 'Marital Status, Life-strains and Depression,' *American Sociological Review*, 42, 5, 704–15.

Penfold, P.S. and Walker, G.A. (1984) *Women and the Psychiatric Paradox*, Milton Keynes: Open University Press.

Piachaud, D. (1984) *Round About 50 Hours a Week*, London: C.P.A.G.

Pitfield, N. (1985) 'Making Gardens from Wildernesses,' in S. Hemmings (ed.) *A Wealth of Experience. The Lives of Older Women*, London: Pandora Press.

Popplestone, E. (1980) 'Top Jobs for Women: Are the Cards Stacked Against Them?,' *Social Work Today*, 12, 4, 12–15.

Prescott, L.F. and Highley, M.S. (1985) 'Drugs Prescribed for Self-poisoners,' *British Medical Journal*, 290, 1 June, 1633–35.

Radloff, L.S. (1980) 'Risk factors for Depression: What Do We Learn from Them?,' in M. Guttentag, S. Salasin and D. Belle (eds) *The Mental Health of Women*, New York: Academic Press.

Rado, F. (1928) 'The Problem of Melancholia,' *International Journal of Psychoanalysis*, 9, 420–38.

Rainwater, J. (1981) *You're in Charge!*, Northamptonshire: Turnstone Press.

Ravetz, J. (1982) 'When Mother Breaks Down,' *Social Work Today*, 13, 21, 14.

Release (1982) *Trouble with Tranquillizers*, London: Release Publications.

Rice, D.G. and Rice, J.K. (1977) 'Non-Sexist "Marital" Therapy,' *Journal of Marriage and Family Counselling*, 3, 1, 3–10.

Rich, C. (1984) 'Ageing, Ageism and Feminist Avoidance,' in B. Macdonald and C. Rich, (1984) *Look Me In The Eye*,

London: The Women's Press.

Richey, C.A. (1981) 'Assertiveness Training for Women,' in S.P. Schinke (ed.) *Behavioral Methods in Social Welfare*, New York: Aldine.

Richman, N. (1974) 'The Effects of Housing on Pre-School Children and their Mothers,' *Developmental Medicine and Child Neurology*, 16, 53–8.

Richman, N. (1977) 'Behaviour Problems in Pre-School Children: Family and Social Factors,' *British Journal of Psychiatry*, 131, 523–7.

Roberts, H. (ed.) (1981) *Doing Feminist Research*, London: Routledge and Kegan Paul.

Roberts, H. (1985) *Patient Patients*, London: Pandora Press.

Robertson, J. (1983) 'Menopause,' *Spare Rib*, 127, 50–5.

Rosenfield, S. (1980) 'Sex Differences in Depression: Do Women Always have Higher Rates?,' *Journal of Health and Social Behavior*, 21, March, 33–42.

Rowe, D. (1983) *Depression: The Way Out of Your Prison*, London: Routledge and Kegan Paul.

Rush, A.J., Beck, A.T., Kovacs, M. and Hollon, S. (1977) 'Comparative Efficacy of Cognitive Therapy and Pharmacotherapy in the Treatment of Depressed Outpatients,' *Cognitive Therapy and Research*, 1, 17–37.

Sanchez, V.C., Lewinsohn, P.M. and Larson, D.W. (1980) 'Assertion Training: Effectiveness in the Treatment of Depression,' Journal of Clinical Psychology, 36, 526–9.

Sanders, D. (1984) *Women and Depression*, London: Sheldon Press.

Scarf, M. (1981) *Unfinished Business*, London: Fontana.

Seligman, M.E.P. (1975) *Helplessness*, San Francisco: Freeman.

Shaw, V. (1983) 'Not Always as Simple as Black and White,' *Community Care*, 4 August, 12–15.

Shepherd, M., Harwin, B.G., Depla, C. and Cairns, V. (1979) 'Social Work and the Primary Care of Mental Disorder,' *Psychological Medicine*, 9, 661–9.

Smith, R. (1982) *Sumitra's Story*, London: The Bodley Head.

Stanway, A. (1981) *Overcoming Depression*, Feltham: Hamlyn.

Stevens, B. (1971) 'The Psychotherapist and Women's Liberation,' *Social Work*, 7, 16, 12–18.

Tatelbaum, J. (1980) *The Courage to Grieve*, London: Heinemann (now available from Gower).

Teasdale, J.D. and Fennel, M.J.V. (1982) 'Immediate Effects

on Depression of Cognitive Therapy Interventions,' *Cognitive Therapy and Research*, 6, 3, 343–52.

Townsend, P. (1979) *Poverty in the UK*, Harmondsworth: Allen Lane/Penguin.

Trower, P., Bryant, B. and Argyle, M. (1978) *Social Skills in Mental Health*, London: Methuen.

Waller, K. (1976) *Social Workers Attitudes to Women*, A report to CCETSW (unpublished).

Warr, P. and Parry, G. (1982) 'Paid Employment and Women's Psychological Well-being,' *Psychological Bulletin*, 91, 498–516.

Weissman, M.M. and Klerman, G.L. (1977) 'Sex Differences in the Epidemiology of Depression,' *Archives of General Psychiatry*, 34, 98–111.

Weissman, M.M., Paykel, E.S. and Klerman, G.L. (1972) 'The Depressed Woman as a Mother,' *Social Psychiatry*, 7, 98–108.

Weissman, M.S. and Paykel, E.S. (1974) *The Depressed Woman: a study of social relationships*, Chicago: University of Chicago Press.

Welburn, V. (1980) *Postnatal Depression*, Glasgow: Fontana.

White, R. (1977) 'Current Psychoanalytic concepts of Depression,' in W. Fann (ed.) *Phenomenology and Treatment of Depression*, New York: Spectrum, 127–41.

Wilson, E. (1977) *Women and the Welfare State*, London: Tavistock Publications.

Wilson, E. (1983) 'Feminism and Social Policy,' in M. Loney, D. Boswell and J. Clarke (eds) *Social Policy and Social Welfare*, Milton Keynes: Open University Press.

Wolfe, J.L. and Fodor, I.G. (1977) 'Modifying Assertive Behavior in Women: A Comparison of Three Approaches,' *Behavior Therapy*, 8, 567–74.

Wolff, S. (1961) 'Social and Family Background of Pre-school Children with Behaviour Disorders Attending a Child-Guidance Clinic,' *Journal of Child Psychology and Psychiatry*, 2, 260–8.

Worden, J.W. (1983) *Grief Counselling and Grief Therapy*, London and New York: Tavistock Publications.

Name Index

Subject Index